DOBSON ON DOBSON
1787–1865

The plate on the picture frame is inscribed as follows: ' "John Dobson (1787–1865). This portrait was presented to Mr Roy and Mr Ian Caller, by Ainsworth Spark Associates, Architects, and Badge Group Design, Graphic Designers, on the occasion of the opening of Linden Hall Hotel, on 6th April, 1981.'

The painting (which is the property of Linden Hall) shows a young man, clearly in his late twenties or early thirties, and is believed to be by J. W. Snow, painted in 1836. It must, therefore, be a copy and not an original work, since by 1836 John Dobson was almost fifty years old – which, obviously, in this painting he is not.

Photograph included by kind permission of Callers-Linden Holdings Limited (Julia C. Marshall, Manager, Linden Hall Hotel, Longhorsley, Morpeth, Northumberland).

Dobson on Dobson

A Photographic Record of Works associated with John Dobson (1787–1865)

DOBSON

The Pentland Press
Edinburgh - Cambridge - Durham - USA

© Dobson, 2000

First published in 2000 by
The Pentland Press Ltd
1 Hutton Close
South Church
Bishop Auckland
Durham

All rights reserved
Unauthorised duplication
contravenes existing laws

ISBN 1-85821-813-6

Typeset in Dante 11/13 by
Carnegie Publishing, Carnegie House, Chatsworth Road, Lancaster
Printed and bound by Bookcraft (Bath) Ltd.

Contents

Acknowledgements ix
Author's Note xii
Introduction 1
The Pineapple Inn, Dobson's Birthplace 8
Bone China Memento of John Dobson 9
Chronological List of Photographs 10–15

PERIOD I 1811–1817 17
Scottish Presbyterian Church, North Shields 19
Newbrough Hall, Hexham 20
Linden Hall, Longhorsley 21
Cheeseburn Grange, Stamfordham 23
North Seaton Hall, Ashington 26
Bradley Hall, Wylam 27
Fallodon Hall, Embleton 29
Unthank Hall, Haltwhistle 32
Prestwick Lodge, Ponteland 33
Backworth Hall, Backworth 36
Minsteracres Monastery (1) 37
(West) Jesmond Towers, Newcastle (1) 38
St Nicholas' Cathedral, Newcastle (1) 40
Nazareth House, Newcastle 41
Tynemouth Castle 41
Axwell Park, Blaydon 42

PERIOD II 1818–1820 45
Doxford Hall, Chathill 47
Church of St John of Beverley, St John Lee, Hexham 49
Wallington Hall, Cambo 50
Belford Hall, Northumberland 51
Gosforth Park, Newcastle 55
St Nicholas' Church, South Gosforth 56
Rock Hall, Alnwick 57
Hebburn Hall, Hebburn 59
Hexham House, Hexham 59
Chipchase Castle, Wark-on-Tyne 60
The Hermitage 63
The Old Rectory (Vicarage), Ponteland 65
The Navigational Beacons, Ross Sands 65
Newton Villa Farm, Felton 67
Thirston House, West Thirston 68
Blagdon Hall, Blagdon 70

South Lodge, Belford Hall, Belford 71

PERIOD III 1821–1829 73
Hawthorn Tower, Hawthorn 75
The Prison, Wooler 76
Flotterton House, Snitter 77
Angerton Hall, Hatburn 78
John Dobson's House, Newcastle 79
Acton House, Felton 80
Sheriff Hill Hall, Gateshead Fell 80
'Thornleigh', 32 Church Road, Low Fell, Gateshead 84
St Nicholas' Cathedral, Newcastle (2) 84
Nunnykirk Hall, Netherwitton 88
The Lying-in Hospital, Newcastle 90
Shawdon Hall, Glanton (1) 90
The Fish Market, Newcastle 91
The Old Vicarage, Haltwhistle 92
(West) Jesmond Towers, Newcastle (2) 93
Bellister Castle 96
The Chantry, Morpeth 98
St Nicholas' Cathedral, Newcastle (3) 100
Mitford Hall, Mitford 101
Longhirst Hall, Morpeth 102
The Church of St Cuthbert, Greenhead 106
High Ford Bridge, Morpeth 107
The Court House, Morpeth 109
St Mary's Parish Church, Belford 122
Lilburn Tower, Alnwick 113
Embleton Old Vicarage, (Now Embleton Towers) 116
The Village Cross, Holy Island 121
St Mary's Place, Newcastle 122
Church of St John the Baptist, Grainger Street, Newcastle 123
Harbottle Castle House, Northumberland 124
The Hall, Glanton Pyke 125

PERIOD IV 1830–1839 127
The Church of St Andrew, Bywell, Stocksfield (1) 129
St Thomas' Crescent, Newcastle 129
Woolsington Hall, Ponteland 130
Church of St Thomas the Martyr, Newcastle 131
Church of St Nicholas, West Boldon 133
Chollerton Grange, Hexham (1) 134
Watergate Building, Newcastle 135
Burnhopeside Hall, Lanchester 136
(14–20) Great North Road, Newcastle 137
Chesters, Humshaugh, Hexham (1) 138
Meldon Park, Hartburn 139
Wynyard Park, Billingham 140
Benwell Tower, Newcastle 141
The 'New Bridge', Morpeth 142
Eldon Square, Newcastle 152

Contents

The Church of St James, Benwell, Newcastle 153
St Nicholas' Cathedral, Newcastle (4) 153
Blenkinsopp Hall, Haltwhistle 156
The Grainger Market, Newcastle 157
Newcastle General Cemetery 158
Low Ford Bridge, Morpeth 160
Grey Street (East Side), Newcastle 161
Brinkburn Priory Church of St Peter and St Paul 161
Brinkburn Priory House, Northumberland 164
Grey Street, 'The Curve', Newcastle 167
Holy Trinity Church, Gateshead 168
Chesters, Humshaugh, Hexham (2) 169
Holme Eden Abbey, Warwick Bridge 171
Grainger Town, Newcastle 173
Nun Street, Newcastle 177
Nelson Street, Newcastle 178
The Cordwainers' Hall, Newcastle 178
Clayton Street, Newcastle 179
Craster Tower, Northumberland 179

PERIOD V 1840–1850 183
Carlton Terrace, Newcastle 185
Boldon House, East Boldon 186
Beaufront Castle, Hexham 186
Trinity House, Newcastle 188
Market Keeper's House, Newcastle 190
St Joseph's R.C. Church, Birtley 193
The Archibald Reed Monument, Newcastle 194
Hackwood House (formerly 'The Hags'), Hexham 195
Minsteracres Monastery, Consett (2) 196
St Andrew's Church, Newcastle 197
Haughton Castle, Hexham 198
The Town Hall, North Shields 201
The Old Vicarage, Chatton (now 'Longstone House') 202
The Church of St Paul, Holme Eden, Warwick Bridge 205
Holme Eden Vicarage, Warwick Bridge 206
The Baptist Church, Howard Street, North Shields 207
Chollerton Grange, Chollerton (2) 208
The Old Vicarage, Stamfordham 208
The Collingwood Monument, Tynemouth 209
The (Castle) Keep, Newcastle 210
The Church of St Cuthbert, Bensham, Gateshead 211
Church of St Mary the Virgin, Stamfordham 212
St John's Church, Grainger Street, Newcastle 213
The Keeper's Cottage, Welton, Horsley-on-the-Hill 214
The Church of St Andrew, Winston on Tees 215
All Saints Church, Monkwearmouth 215
The Church of St John the Baptist, Meldon 216
The Church of St Peter, Bywell 217
Central Station, Newcastle (1) 218
Church of the Holy Trinity, Embleton 219

Church of St Cuthbert, Benfieldside 220
The Church of St Andrew, Bywell (2) 221

PERIOD VI 1851–1865 223
The Barber Surgeons' Hall, Newcastle 225
Almshouses, Hospital of St Mary the Virgin, Newcastle 225
The (Royal) Station Hotel, Newcastle 226
Benfieldside Vicarage, Shotley Bridge 227
Newton Hall, Stocksfield 229
The Percy Chapel, Tynemouth 230
The Leazes, Hexham 232
Church of St Michael and All Angels, Ford 235
Church of St Mary, Gateshead 239
The (Castle) Keep, Newcastle (2) 240
St John's Church, Grainger Street, Newcastle (3) 242
Wallington Hall, Cambo, Morpeth 242
Holy Trinity Vicarage, Seghill 244
St John's Church, Otterburn 245
St Columba's Presbyterian Church, North Shields 245
Chatton Bridge, Chatton 246
The Mechanics' Institute, North Shields 247
Hexham Abbey, Hexham 247
Holeyn Hall, Wylam 249
Shawdon Hall, Glanton, Alnwick (2) 250
Church of St Paul, High Elswick, Newcastle 253
The Parish Church of St Michael and All Angels, Houghton-le-Spring 254
Cathedral Church of St Nicholas, Newcastle (5) 255
Church of St John the Baptist, Newcastle (4) 256
Unthank Hall, Haltwhistle (2) 257
Church of St Lawrence, Warkworth 258
Church of St Gregory, Kirknewton 258
Jesmond Parish Church, Newcastle 259
Lambton Castle, Chester-le-Street 261
Central Station, Newcastle (2) 264
John Dobson's Death 265
Mr Dobson's Funeral 267
Tributes 268

ADDENDA 273
Bolton Hall, Bolton, Alnwick 275
The Old Vicarage ('Mill Race House') Netherwitton 276
Bibliography 279
Index of Buildings Illustrated 281

Acknowledgements

To write a book of this sort without the wholehearted co-operation of others would be an impossible undertaking.

I am greatly indebted to the many authors from whose books I have drawn informed and technical descriptions, particularly Tom Faulkner, Andrew Greg, Nikolaus Pevsner and Lyall Wilkes.

But there are very many other people whose small, but nevertheless valuable, contribution does not appear in my list of acknowledgements (which, rightly or wrongly, confines itself to those whose properties I have photographed), but whose efforts on my behalf I acknowledge and deeply appreciate.

The degree of kindness and generosity of spirit I have encountered throughout both my researches and my travels has overwhelmed me. I am indeed indebted to so many for their interest, their patience and simply their help.

It has been a joy to photograph so many splendid buildings, both private and public, but equally it has been a privilege and a pleasure to meet so many wonderful people.

Newbrough Hall (near Hexham), Mr W. A. Benson. Linden Hall (Longhorsley), Mrs Julia C. Marshall. Cheesburn Grange (Stamfordham), Captain and Mrs S. F. Riddell. North Seaton Hall (near Ashington), Wansbeck District Council, Mrs K. Mavin, Executive Manager. Bradley Hall (Wylam), Mr and Mrs R. M. C. Simpson. Fallodon Hall (Embleton, near Alnwick), Mr Peter O. R. Bridgeman. Unthank Hall (Haltwhistle), Mr and Mrs W. R. Webster. Prestwick Lodge (Ponteland), Mr and Mrs Michael Wilson. Backworth Hall (Killingworth), The Committee and Secretary of the Miners' Welfare. Minsteracres (Retreat Centre, Consett), Revd. Aelred Smith. West Jesmond Towers, now La Sagesse High School (North Jesmond, Newcastle), Mrs Linda Clark, Head Teacher. Nazareth House, formerly Sandyford Park and Villa Real (Sandyford Road, Newcastle), The Poor Sisters of Nazareth and Mr Mark McKelvey, Lamb and Edge, Chartered Surveyors, Pilgrim Street, Newcastle. Doxford Hall (Chathill), Mr and Mrs Brian Burnie. Belford Hall and Lodge (Belford), Mr Alan Graham, Chairman, Belford Hall Management Co. Ltd. Rock Hall (Rock, near Alnwick), Mr C. J. Bosanquet. Hexham House (Hexham), Mr Alan Batey, Chief Executive, Tynedale Council. Sheriff Hill Hall (Low Fell, near Gateshead), Gateshead Central Library. Hebburn Hall (Hebburn), Mr R. S. Carr-Ellison and the Ellison Hall Masonic Club (East Wing) and Mr David McKenna (West Wing). Chipchase Castle (Wark on Tyne), Mrs P. J. Torday. The Hermitage (Hexham), Mr L. G. Allgood. The Old Rectory (Ponteland), Mr Philip G. Walton. The Navigational Beacons (Guile Point, Ross

Sands) and Trinity House (Broad Chare, Quayside, Newcastle), The Brethren of Trinity House, Captain Rennison Shipley. Newton Villa Farm (Felton, near Morpeth), Mr and Mrs David N. O. Scott. Thirston House (Felton, near Morpeth), Mr and Mrs Brian Reed. Blagdon Hall (Seaton Burn), The Hon. Matthew White Ridley. Flotterton House (Thropton, Rothbury, near Morpeth), Mr F. T. Walton. Angerton Hall (Hartburn, near Morpeth), Mr and Mrs T. E. Stephens. Acton House (Felton, near Morpeth), Mr and Mrs D. M. Moore. Nunnykirk Hall (Netherwitton, near Morpeth), Mr S. Dalby-Ball, Headmaster. The Lying-in Hospital, now Portland House (New Bridge Street, Newcastle) The Newcastle Building Society. Shawdon Hall Lodges (Glanton, near Alnwick), Major R. F. H. Cowan. The Old Vicarage (Haltwhistle), Mr Colin Creighton. The Chantry (Bridge Street, Morpeth), Castle Morpeth Borough Council, Environmental and Planning Services, Mrs Dawn Goodwill-Evans, Tourism Officer. Mitford Hall and Lodge (Mitford, near Morpeth), Mr B. S. Shepherd. Longhirst Hall (Longhirst, near Morpeth), Mr David Williamson. Woolsington Hall (Woolsington, near Newcastle), Cameron Hall Developments Limited. The Court House (Morpeth), Chesterton International Property Consultants. Lilburn Tower (near Alnwick), Mr Duncan Davidson. Embleton Towers, formerly The Vicarage (Embleton, near Alnwick), Mr K. J. Seymour-Walker. Harbottle Castle House (Harbottle, Rothbury, near Morpeth), Mr and Mrs J. E. Wilson. The Hall, Glanton Pyke (Glanton, near Alnwick, Mr and Mrs John S. R. Swanson. Chollerton Grange, formerly the Vicarage (Chollerton, near Hexham), 'The Owner'. The Watergate Building (Sandhill, Newcastle), Home Housing Association 1998 Ltd., Mr Colin Garbutt, Regional Manager. Burnhopeside Hall (Lanchester), Mrs Christine Hewitt. Benwell Tower, formerly 'The Mitre' (Benwell, Newcastle), The British Broadcasting Corporation. Wynyard Park (Billingham), Cameron Hall Developments Limited (Sir John and Lady Hall). Meldon Park (Meldon, near Morpeth), Mr M. J. B. Cookson. Chesters (Humshaugh), Mr George Benson. Blenkinsopp Hall (Haltwhistle), Mrs M. L. Joicey. Holme Eden Abbey (Warwick Bridge, near Carlisle), Mrs Doreen H. Parsons. Craster Tower, Craster, near Alnwick), Mrs J. M. Craster and Miss M. D. Cra'ster. Beaufront Castle (Hexham), and Sandhoe House (Hexham), Mr J. Aidan Cuthbert. The Market Keeper's House (Scotswood Road, Newcastle), Tyne and Wear Development Corporation. Hackwood House, formerly 'The Hags' (Hexham), Mr and Mrs R. W. Wassell. Haughton Castle (Humshaugh, near Hexham), 'The Owner'. Holme Eden Vicarage (St. Paul's, Warwick Bridge, near Carlisle), The Revd. J. S. Casson. The Old Vicarage (Stamfordham), Mr and Mrs I. H. Nicholson. Castle Keep (Newcastle), The Society of Antiquaries. Welton Keeper's Cottage (Horsley-on-the-Hill), Northumbrian Water. The Royal Station Hotel (Neville Street, Newcastle), Mr Arvin Handa. Mowden Hall School, formerly Newton Hall (Newton, near Stocksfield), Mr Andrew P. Lewis, Headmaster. The Leazes (Hexham), Mr John E. Knipe and Dr George Ward. The Old Vicarage (Seghill), Mr Colin Lawson. Holeyn Hall (Wylam), Dr and Mrs John Williams and Drs W.

Acknowledgements

and A. Brough. Lambton Castle (Chester-le-Street), The Lambton Estate, Mr Robert Kirton-Darling, Estate Manger. Bolton Hall (West Bolton, near Alnwick), Mr and Mrs J. Hylton Young. The Old Vicarage, now Mill Race House (Netherwitton, near Morpeth), Mrs J. C. R. Trevelyan.

Addenda

Boldon House (East Boldon, near Sunderland), Mr Donald Graham. 32 Church Road, formerly the wing of Sheriff Hill Hall (Low Fell, near Gateshead), Mr and Mrs Duncan Smith. East and West Longstone House, formerly The Old Vicarage (Chatton), Dr Stephen and Mrs Spoor and Mr Robert and Mrs H. K. Handyside. Hawthorn Tower (Near Easington Village, Peterlee, County Durham), Easington District Council.

English Heritage kindly gave their permission to photograph the following properties:

Brinkburn Priory and House (Rothbury near Morpeth); The Percy Chapel (Tynemouth Priory), the Priory itself and the fortifications of the Castle.

The National Trust likewise allowed me to photograph the following properties:

Wallington Hall (Wallington, near Morpeth); Bellister Castle (near Haltwhistle).

Author's Note

At the outset of writing two crucial factors had to be considered: firstly, which subjects were to be included in this reference to Dobson's work and secondly, how were they to be arranged?

Eventually it was decided on a basis of degree. Photographs of those buildings which had a rather tenuous association with the architect must, sadly, be discarded and only those with a substantial connection should be retained. Natually this meant that much of Dobson's earlier work, important though it was, but where his contribution was relatively minimal, 'went by the board'. As his career progressed and his reputation became established, there is, in the nature of things, much more evidence to illustrate the extent of his involvement.

As to the arrangement of contents, I had three reasonable options: the subjects should be listed alphabetically; they could be set out under group headings, i.e. country houses, churches, castles, monuments etc.; or they could be arranged chronologically.

This latter seemed the most logical and sensible course since, theoretically at least, it would hopefully indicate to the reader Mr Dobson's progression in style, thinking and in his ideas, over the half-century of his working life.

Since I have strictly observed this method throughout the book, it does mean that some subjects 'crop up' more than once, with a gap of several years between features. However, I have taken care never to use the same photograph twice, thus ensuring that on each occasion the reader views a different aspect of the building concerned.

Finally, in deference to those who may wish to find a particular building quickly and easily, a simple Index of Buildings Illustrated has been appended.

Introduction

My interest in the life and work of John Dobson was first aroused more than twenty years ago, when, with a group of young students, I was conducting a more general study of 18th c. and 19th c. well-known Northumbrian characters. Among those we examined were Lord Charles ('Reform Bill') Grey; Robert 'Chinese' Morrison; George and Robert Stephenson, William Hedley and Daniel Gooch, the railway engineers; Josephine Butler, the social reformer; Thomas Atthey, the fossils expert; Admiral Lord Cuthbert Collingwood, Nelson's second-in-command at the Battle of Trafalgar; Grace Darling, of Farne Island fame; and, of course, Thomas Bewick, the great engraver.

All of these (and many more) are fascinating subjects in their own right, full of interest and equally worthy of careful individual study, but it was John Dobson who seized my curiosity.

I can only suppose it was, in part at least, because so much of Dobson's work still exists to be seen, admired and appreciated that 'gave him an edge' over the others.

I have no architectural training or background and so in this respect I am unqualified to appreciate the finer points of Dobson's work.

Mine is simply an interest and an aesthetic appreciation – rather (if you will) like the layman in an art gallery, regarded, perhaps, by the 'cognoscenti' as an ignorant philistine, unable to understand the finer techniques of a painting, but who stubbornly claims to 'know what he likes' and who is distinctly unimpressed by what his 'betters' consider 'good'.

Unfortunately I lack the necessary technical knowledge to make an informed judgement of what is 'good' architecture: nevertheless, I, too, 'know what I like'. When, therefore, I hear criticism of some of Dobson's work, I rightly, or wrongly, assume the criticism is valid since those making it have the technical qualifications which I do not.

Like many other people, however, I tend to view critics with the same suspicion I reserve for 'experts'. We all know the value of constructive criticism, since we can profit from it; but all too often those who see fit to criticise the work or the efforts of others are no more than individuals overwhelmed by an exaggerated belief in their own opinions and importance, and are wont to malign and denigrate while unable to offer anything reasonable or reasoned themselves. Such criticism is not only unhelpful and unworthy but entirely without value. Even my limited understanding of the finer points of architecture accepts that every piece of Dobson's work cannot be judged perfect. He was, nevertheless, as Gervase Jackson-Stops described him in *Country Life* (edition of February 5th,

1976), '... one of the most accomplished architects ever to have practised outside London ... in no way a provincial and his work is consistently more interesting and more accomplished than many of his better known contemporaries.' He was (as Lyall Wilkes describes him in *Tyneside Portraits*) 'a modest and unassuming man who devoted his life wholly to architecture and the arts'. Had he decided to practise his 'art' in London, as many of his friends so strongly suggested, there seems little doubt he would have been a nationally rather than a regionally recognised success. Perhaps he lacked a certain necessary ambition, or confidence – or both.

On the other hand, had he listened to these 'siren voices' and paid heed to their overtures and had he, indeed, established his career in 'the great metropolis', then the City of Newcastle and the County of Northumberland, in particular, would have been so very much the poorer as a result. The more I read of Dobson, the more I was intrigued by the man.

It would be romantic, but, in truth, rather ridiculous, to describe him as 'a poor boy made good', for frankly this is an image far removed from reality. His father (John Dobson Senior) was a man of substance – he owned a public house and was a gardener and nurseryman on a considerable scale.

Dobson's early years, therefore, were certainly not a struggle: compared to many of his contemporaries, John Dobson's was a comfortable existence. His parents were concerned that their son should make a success of his life and gave him every practical support and encouragement to achieve that end. Whatever talents he inherited from his parents, talents nourished and developed partly through their concerns and attentions and partly through the help he received from others, the fact remains, he was a gifted child who, largely through his innate abilities, his perseverance and his exceptional dedication, became a gifted adult. Not only did he become 'one of the most important architects of the first half of the nineteenth century ... and a very fine designer in the Classical manner and in the Gothic style, he was also a notable innovator in structural design' (Lyall Wilkes).

He was a fine water-colourist. His early training as a gardener served him in admirable stead on numerous occasions. Indeed it was sometimes said, with perhaps more than a grain of justification and truth, that 'he almost preferred the landscape and gardens to the building itself' (Faulkner and Greg).

Dobson-designed furniture 'is as ingenious as it is striking' (Lyall Wilkes): in short, there is so much to admire and capture one's interest in the life and work of this 'man of many parts'.

Without any formal or even recognisable qualification, it would have been presumptuous of me to try and write any kind of assessment of, or commentary on, the quality of John Dobson's architecture. Instead, I decided at the outset that my small tribute to the genius of my illustrious namesake would take the form of a photographic recognition of the surviving works associated with this formidable character.

Introduction

Even so, my photographs are patently amateur. I possess none of the expensive, sophisticated equipment so essential to the professional photographer. Photography for me, as it is for countless thousands of others, is simply a hobby which I enjoy and which affords me (and them) a great deal of pleasure. I see the work of professional photographers and I blush at my temerity; for I am under no illusion that my unworthy efforts bear any comparison. I ask, therefore, that my humble offerings be kindly judged, but strictly within the parameters of the definition 'amateur', for I, more than my severest critic, am aware of the limitations and shortcomings of my technical expertise.

Over the past five years, as opportunities have allowed, I have photographed and often re-photographed Dobson's surviving works. To that end I have travelled hundreds of miles, in Northumberland, Durham and Cumbria, covering all four points of the compass.

During these, and indeed the previous years, it has been my real privilege to meet scores of interesting people who have shown me trust, great warmth and incredible hospitality. In all that time I have only twice been refused permission to take photographs and in both instances there were perfectly valid reasons for the refusal – a refusal given courteously and, I suspect, with genuine regret.

That so many others should have tolerated the boyish enthusiasm of a total stranger to the extent they did, is quite remarkable and a cause of real astonishment to me. That they should so readily, and often eagerly, have shown such friendliness, so far beyond what I had hoped for, has placed me forever in their debt.

Some good souls invited me into their homes. Others diligently searched for papers and records to assist my researches. Almost all have given me freedom to wander unsupervised through grounds and gardens, 'snapping' at will. Some have written to or telephoned third parties on my behalf; one young lady placed her college thesis entirely at my disposal!

All have given me their time and support and shown a keen interest in my work. I must, of course, readily and happily acknowledge those who have kindly given me permission to photograph their properties.

It would, alas, be impossible to mention all who have given me their assistance, however great the temptation; but whether they work in shops or offices, libraries or schools; whether they live in fine houses, castles or lodges, rectories or old vicarages, I am immensely indebted to each and every one of them for their patience, their help and their inestimable kindness.

The purpose of this book is simply to record (through the medium of photography), as much as I am able, the remaining works with which John Dobson is associated.

Its pages illustrate, I hope and believe, the marvellous versatility of this shy, kindly, genial, honest and prodigious craftsman. Sadly, over the period of the last thirty years or so, in and around the City of Newcastle and in the neighbouring County of Northumberland (and even further afield), much of John Dobson's work has been lost forever. Warehouses, gaols and schools (including the Clergy Jubilee School, Carliol Square, and the Royal Jubilee School, City Road) have disappeared. Many private residences have fallen victim to the hammer, the bulldozer, the mechanical shovel and the developer's dream: Picton House, High Cross House; Jesmond Park, Jesmond Grove and Gresham Place; North Seaton Hall, Cramlington Hall, Swansfield House and Broome Park: Preston Villa, Hylton Lodge, Waterville House and West Chirton House: Sudbrooke Holme in Lincolnshire and Oatlands House, Weybridge in Surrey – all are no more.

His churches too have not escaped unscathed: St James' in Blackett Street; St Peter's, Oxford Street and the Wesleyan Church on New Road – all gone. The Church of the Divine Unity and the Church of the Holy Trinity on New Bridge Street; the Presbyterian Church on Frederick Street, South Shields; St Paul's, Hendon, Sunderland and St Mary's, Tyne Dock – none will ever again accommodate worshippers or be a focal point for their local communities. Public buildings have shared the same fate: the Royal Arcade (described by Faulkner and Greg as 'one of Dobson's most dignified compositions') is now but a replica of Dobson's original. Eldon Square has been vandalised to make way for a shopping centre – only the east side of these once fashionable terraces remains. The Infirmary on Forth Street, the offices of the *Newcastle Courant* in George Yard and the Freemasons' Lodge in Middlesbrough have all been 'erased' by developers.

This is a truly depressing list, the more so because it is by no means complete. These are examples only of a much longer inventory of buildings John Dobson designed, built, restored or altered during a long, successful and exemplary career – and others may even now be under threat. Hopefully, most, if not all, of those featured here will survive well into the next century and beyond ... surely John Dobson deserves no less.

My sources for information on buildings which have been destroyed are, largely, as follows:

Lost Houses of Newcastle and Northumberland, Thomas Faulkner & Phoebe Lowery.
John Dobson, Newcastle Architect, 1787–1865, Thomas Faulkner & Andrew Greg.
John Dobson, Architect and Landscape Gardener, Lyall Wilkes. I am indebted to these authors.

John Dobson was born at Chirton, North Shields (on December 9th), in 1787. At a very early age he showed a remarkable talent for drawing; and amusing stories are told of the wrath of the villagers, which was often roused on finding their gates and shutters decorated with sketches in chalk by his furtive hand.

Mr Lawson, the village schoolmaster, perceiving his bent, gave him a set of drawing materials whereupon he ceased his 'al fresco' efforts. He must have advanced quickly in skill as he was, while still a child, appointed to the office of 'Honorary Draftsman' to Mr McClashan, a celebrated damask weaver in the neighbourhood, and actually, at the early age of eleven or twelve, executed designs which were of valuable assistance to Mr McClashan in his trade.

Introduction

His father, who appears to have been a man of considerable ability and judgement, wisely determined to give his son the advantage of a thoroughly good English education and granted him every facility to pursue his studies after leaving the hands of Mr Lawson.

At the age of fifteen, the boy was placed by his father as a pupil with Mr David Stephenson, who was, at that time, the leading builder and architect in Newcastle.

In this office he made rapid progress and gained a thorough knowledge of architecture. He learned not only to draw a plan but to see it executed, and he even acquired an unusual acquaintance with carpentry and masonry. During this time he also studied surveying with a Mr Hall of Stamfordham. In these aesthetic days some might perhaps consider this practical training beneath the dignity of the profession.

Painting of John Dobson

On this point we need only remember the regrets expressed by the eminent French architect, Monsieur Viollet le Duc, as to the superficial character of his own early experience. He tells us that for two years he was set to copy drawings of buildings, of which he was told neither the age nor the country nor the use; that he then worked for so much an hour in an architect's office, tracing plans and nothing else, except now and then to make some detailed drawings, not knowing how, never having seen the smallest part of a building executed.

During the time Mr Dobson was in Mr Stephenson's office, he became a pupil of Mr Boniface Moss, an Italian refugee (brother of the celebrated enamel painter), by whom he was instructed in the arts of fencing, perspective and enamel painting. In 1810, John Dobson completed his studies with Stephenson, on whose advice he decided to establish himself in Newcastle, strictly as an architect. Before commencing his profession, however, he resolved to seek instruction from John Varley, 'the father of English water-colour drawing', and with this intention proceeded to London.

On his arrival he found the realisation of his wishes attended with greater difficulty than he had anticipated. Varley declined to be troubled with young pupils and at first declared that he could not spare even half an hour. Observing, however, the intense disappointment of the youth, he at last consented to give him lessons at five in the morning, his time during the day being fully occupied. This concession, made at some inconvenience, marked the recognition of a kindred spirit.

The master soon perceived the uncommon qualities of his pupil and not only agreed to give him daily instruction, but invited him to lodge at his house and would hardly part with him when, six weeks later, suitable lodgings were found.

A mutual esteem sprang up which continued in after-life. Varley and his pupil worked all day together but, curious to relate, the labours of the master were interrupted from time to time to calculate the nativity and draw the horoscope of some lady of fashion, for Varley was an amateur astrologer in his lighter moments.

During this first visit to London, Mr Dobson formed lasting friendships with numerous eminent men, among whom were Turner, William Hunt, Mulready, West, Robert Smirke, Professor Donaldson and others.

In the early part of his career he also formed a friendship with his future son-in-law, Sydney Smirke R.A., an intimacy which grew with years and was life-long. During the whole of this protracted period they were constantly in the habit of consulting one another, comparing notes and exchanging sketches. This correspondence, so full of interest from an architectural point of view, is unfortunately lost, the few letters that now remain being only of a trivial nature. This is truly to be regretted.

Robert Smirke strongly urged Mr Dobson to establish himself as an architect in London. Had he followed this advice, no doubt he would have had a great career, but his nature was retiring and he shrank from what appeared too great an enterprise for one so young. When, contrary to the advice of his friends, he returned to Newcastle, although he was (with the exception of Mr Bonomi of Durham), the only professional architect between Edinburgh and York, he soon discovered that the demand for his services had to be created. He found what many young men have experienced, that it is easier to profess an art than to practise it.

An architect's advice was in but little request, and to one so young and unknown engagements came but slowly. Like a true artist, he never allowed himself to be idle for want of work. In the intervals of unemployment he travelled in England and France, assiduously studying and sketching castellated and church architecture, a habit which he continued to the end of his life.

Mr Dobson sometimes beguiled his leisure hours by designing for the stage, and it may interest some to know that he composed and drew in perspective a celebrated drop-scene for the old Theatre of Newcastle.

He also drew the proscenium for the Newcastle Theatre, in which the Royal Arms were so perfect in perspective that even competent draughtsmen often took them to be in relievo.

His strong and robust frame, together with his untiring industry, enabled Mr

Introduction

Dobson to accomplish an enormous amount of work. His habit of early rising, which he retained throughout his life, was the wonder of a Frenchman, whose rooms were opposite to his office. This gentleman would often exclaim – 'On parle de l'homme sans ombre, mais voici un qui ne dort jamais.'

His hours of rising were four or five in the morning and his remarkable power of doing without sleep enabled him constantly to work until twelve at night. In the year 1859 Mr Dobson became President of the Northern Architectural Association.

Mr Dobson married the eldest daughter of Alexander Rutherford of Warburton House, Gateshead-on-Tyne, a lady of great artistic talent, her miniature painting being far beyond ordinary amateur work.

They had three sons and five daughters. The eldest son, the late John Dobson, assisted his father for some years in office work. The eldest daughter married the late Sydney Smirke R.A. One son and three daughters died in childhood. The youngest son, Alexander Ralph, inherited all his father's artistic genius. While studying his profession in the office of Mr Sydney Smirke, he gained the first prize at University College, London, for Architecture (Fine Arts); also the first prize in Architecture (Construction).

He had just returned to his father's office, full of youthful enthusiasm for his art, when he met his sad fate in the explosion at Gateshead, on October 4th 1854.

Of men like Mr Dobson, apart from their professional life, there is little to be said that can be of interest to the general reader. The man of productive genius can only be known through his works, and this, which is true of all, is especially true of the architect.

His works (unlike those of the painter or musician), are to be found at great distances from one another and only figured representations of them can be brought together. He matures his designs in the privacy of his home and when they are put in execution, we see the mason and the joiner at work, not the architect. The characteristics of great architects are less known, their names are more easily forgotten, than those of any other of the tribe of artists. The designers of many of the noblest buildings of the world have been lost to fame. It may be added that the architect is more liable to disappointments from baffled enterprise than those engaged any other profession. He has to contend with the wills and prejudices of others; he is hampered by committees, and the designs by which he expected to become famous are often either cut down for want of means or, perhaps, altogether abandoned.

Mr Dobson had many such trials to overcome; but his elevated love of his art never failed to surmount all depressing incidents.

Few men ever spent so long a life in so laborious a manner, having gained the love and esteem of all who knew them. It would be difficult to overpraise his generous, genial, simple, warm-hearted, honourable nature.

The long and honoured life of John Dobson reached its close on January 8th,

1865. He died at his residence in New Bridge Street, Newcastle, in his seventy-seventh year.

For the want of a more accurate, informed, colourful and detailed account of the life of John Dobson, I have taken these extracts (verbatim) from the book written (with obvious pride and pleasure) by his daughter, Margaret Jane – published as her *Memoir* of her father, in 1885.

There is not, to my knowledge, a more accurate, albeit brief, account of his life to be read anywhere.

It must be added, however, that the same degree of accuracy does not always relate to the list of his works found in the *Memoir* – but that is another story!

The Pineapple Inn *(High Chirton, North Shields)*
Photograph taken in August, 1997.

(John Dobson was born here on December the 9th, 1787.)

Introduction

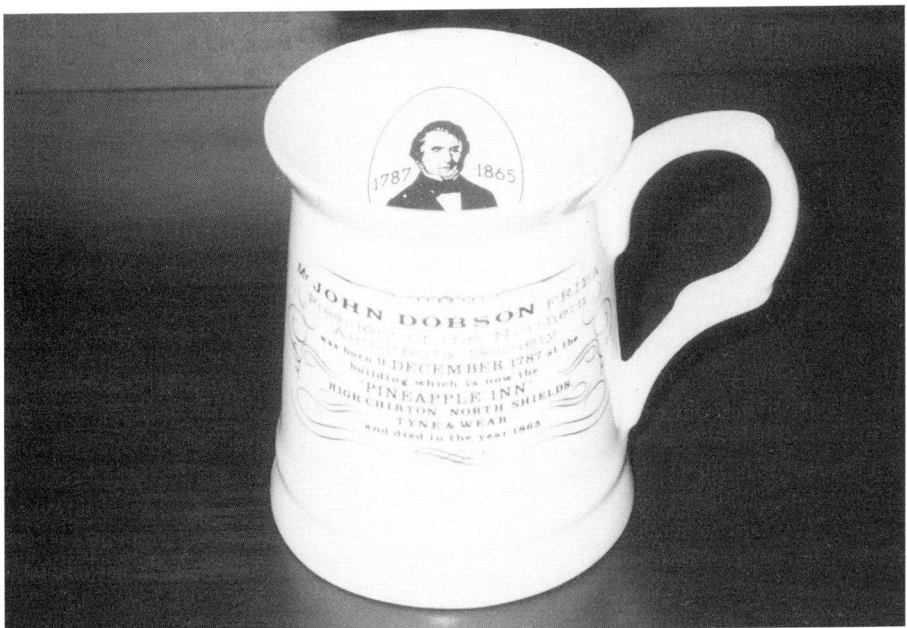

Bone china memento of John Dobson

Among the souvenirs produced in 1987 to celebrate the bi-centenary of John Dobson's birth (in 1787) was this bone china memento, purchased at the Laing Art Gallery, Newcastle, and suitably inscribed with a very brief summary of the architect's life and work.

A Chronological List

The Photographs relating to John Dobson's work (1811–63), including 'John Dobson and the Streets of Grainger Town'.

The Scotch Church (North Shields)	1811
Newbrough Hall	1812
Linden Hall	1812–13
North Seaton Hall	1813
Bradley Hall	1813
Cheeseburn Grange	1813
Gibside Hall	1814
Fallodon Hall	1815
Unthank Hall	1815
Prestwick Lodge	1815
Backworth Hall	1815
Minsteracres	1816
All Saints Church (Newcastle)	1816
(West) Jesmond Towers (now La Sagesse High School, Newcastle)	1817
Cathedral Church of St Nicholas (installation of stoves)	1817
Nazareth House (formerly 'Villa Real', Sandyford Road, Newcastle)	1817
Tynemouth Castle (fortifications)	1817
Axwell Park	1817
Doxford Hall	1818
The Church of St John of Beverley (St John Lee, near Hexham)	1818
Wallington Hall	1818
Belford Hall	1818
The Entrance Gates to Gosforth Park	1818
The Church of St Nicholas (South Gosforth)	1818
Rock Hall	1819
Hexham Abbey House	1819
Hebburn Hall	1819

Chronological List of Dobson's Work

Chipchase Castle	1819
The Hermitage (Hexham)	1819
Cheeseburn Grange	1819
The Old Rectory (Ponteland)	1820
The Navigational Beacons (Guile Point, Ross Sands, near Holy Island)	1820
Newton Villa Farm (Felton, near Morpeth)	c. 1820
Thirston House (West Thirston, Felton, near Morpeth)	c. 1820
Blagdon Hall	c. 1820
South Lodge (Belford Hall)	c. 1820
Hawthorn Tower (Easington Village, County Durham)	1821
Belford 'Prison'	1823
Flotterton House (Rothbury, near Morpeth)	1823
Angerton Hall (Hartburn, near Morpeth)	1823
John Dobson's House (49, New Bridge Street, Newcastle)	1823
Acton House (Felton, near Morpeth)	1823
Sheriff Hill Hall (32, Church Road, Low Fell, Gateshead)	1823–24
Cathedral Church of St Nicholas (Newcastle: north transept window)	1823–24
Nunnykirk Hall (Netherwitton, near Morpeth)	1825
The Lying-in-Hospital, now Portland House (New Bridge Street, Newcastle)	1825
Shawdon Hall	1825
The Fishmarket (Guildhall, Sandhill, Newcastle)	1823–26
The Old Vicarage (Haltwhistle)	1826
(West) Jesmond Towers (now La Sagesse High School, Newcastle)	1823–27
Bellister Castle	1826–27
The Chantry (Morpeth)	1827
Cathedral Church of St Nicholas (Newcastle: rest'n of the steeple)	1827
Mitford Hall (including Lodge)	1823–28
Longhirst Hall	1824–28
The Church of St Cuthbert (Greenhead)	1826–28
The Abbey Church of St Andrew (Hexham: east window)	1828
Woolsington Hall	1828
The High Ford Bridge (Morpeth)	1828

The Court House (Morpeth)	1828
The Church of St Mary (Belford)	1828
Lilburn Tower	1828
Embleton Towers	1828
The Market Cross (Holy Island)	1828
St Mary's Place (Newcastle)	1829
The Church of St John (Newcastle: restoration of chancel and gables)	1829
Harbottle Castle House	1829
The Hall (Glanton Pyke, Glanton, near Alnwick)	1829
The Church of St Andrew (Bywell, Stockfield, near Hexham)	1830
St Thomas' Crescent (Newcastle)	1820–30
The Church of St Thomas the Martyr (Haymarket, Newcastle)	1827–30
The Church of St Nicholas (West Boldon: addition of gallery)	1830
Chollerton Grange (Chollerton, near Hexham)	1830
The Watergate Building (Sandhill, Newcastle)	c. 1830
Burnhopeside Hall (Lanchester, County Durham)	c. 1830
14–20 Great North Road (Newcastle)	1830s
Eldon Square (Newcastle)	1825–31
The 'New Bridge' (referred to as 'the Telford Bridge', Morpeth)	1829–31
Benwell Tower (formerly 'The Mitre', Benwell, Newcastle)	1831
Wynyard Park	1832
Meldon Park	1832
Chesters	1832
The Church of St James (Benwell, Newcastle)	1832
Cathedral Church of St Nicholas (Newcastle: addition of north & south porches)	1832–34
Cathedral Church of St Nicholas (Newcastle: repairs to lantern tower)	1832–34
Blenkinsopp Hall	1835
The Butcher & Vegetable Markets (Grainger Street, Newcastle)	1835
The Low Ford Bridge (Morpeth)	1836
The General Cemetery (Jesmond)	1834–36
The Former Martin's Bank (Grey Street, Newcastle)	1836
Brinkburn Priory Church	1830–37

Chronological List of Dobson's Work

Brinkburn Priory House	1830–37
The East Side of Grey Street (Newcastle)	1835–37
The Church of The Holy Trinity (Gateshead)	1836–37
Chesters	1837
Holme Eden Abbey	1837
The Grainger Market and Street Façades (Newcastle)	1835–38
Nun Street (Newcastle)	1835–38
Nelson Street (Newcastle)	1835–38
The Gaiety Theatre (Newcastle)	1838
Dispensary (Fruit Exchange) (Newcastle)	1838
Cordwainers' Hall (Newcastle)	1838
Clayton Street (Newcastle)	1835–38
Craster Tower	1839
Carlton Terrace (Jesmond Road, Newcastle)	1840
East Boldon House	1840
Beaufront Castle	1837–41
Trinity House	1841
The Market Keeper's House (Scotswood Road, Newcastle)	1841
The R.C. Church of St Joseph (Birtley)	1842–43
The Archibald Reed Monument (Jesmond Cemetery, Newcastle)	1843
Hackwood House (formerly 'the Hags', Hexham)	1843
Minsteracres (the R.C. Church of St Elizabeth)	1843
The Church of St Andrew (Newcastle: addition of south transept window)	1844
Haughton Castle	1844–45
The Town Hall (North Shields)	1844–45
The Old Vicarage (Chatton, near Wooler)	1845
The Church of St Paul (Warwick Bridge, near Carlisle)	1845
St Paul's Vicarage (Warwick Bridge, near Carlisle)	1845
Sandhoe House (Hexham)	1845
The Baptist Church (Howard Street, North Shields)	1846
Chollerton Grange	1847
The Old Vicarage (Stamfordham)	1847
The Collingwood Monument (Tynemouth)	1847
The Castle Keep (Newcastle)	1847

The Church of St Cuthbert (Gateshead)	1845–48
The Church of St Mary (Stamfordham)	1848
The Church of St John (Newcastle: rest'n of west side & porch)	1848
Welton, Keeper's Cottage (Horsley-on-the-Hill)	1848
The Church of St Andrew (Winston, County Durham)	1848
All Saints Church (Monkwearmouth)	1846–49
The Church of St John (Meldon)	1849
The Church of St Peter (Bywell)	1849
The Central Railway Station (Newcastle)	1847–50
The Church of the Holy Trinity (Embleton)	1849–50
The Church of St Cuthbert (Benfieldside, Shotley Bridge)	1849–50
The Church of St Andrew (Bywell)	1850
The Barber-Surgeons' Hall (Victoria Street, Newcastle)	1850–51
The Almshouses (Hospital of St Mary the Virgin, Rye Hill, Newcastle)	1851
The Royal Station Hotel (Neville Street, Newcastle)	1851
St Cuthbert's Vicarage (Benfieldside, Shotley Bridge)	1851
Mowden Hall School (formerly Newton Hall, Stocksfield)	1851
The Percy Chapel (Tynemouth Priory)	1852
The Church of St Michael and All Angels (Ford)	1852–53
The Leazes (Hexham)	1853
The Church of St Mary (Gateshead)	1854–55
The Castle Keep (Newcastle)	1855
The Church of St John (Newcastle: refilled the chancel)	1855
Wallington Hall	1855
The Old Vicarage (Seghill)	1856
The Church of St John (Otterburn)	1855–57
The Church of St Columba (North Shields)	1856–57
Chatton Bridge (Chatton, Northumberland)	1857
The Mechanics' Institute (North Shields)	1857–58
The Abbey Church of St Andrew (Hexham: east window)	1858
Holeyn Hall (Wylam)	1858
Shawdon Hall	1858
The Lodges (Shawdon Hall)	1858
The Church of St Paul (Elswick, Newcastle)	1857–59

Chronological List of Dobson's Work

The Church of St Michael (Houghton-le-Spring, County Durham)	1858–59
The Cathedral Church of St Nicholas (Newcastle: east end)	1859
The Church of St John (Newcastle: altar railings and reredos)	1859
Unthank Hall (Haltwhistle)	1860
The Church of St Lawrence (Warkworth)	1860
The Church of St Gregory (Kirknewton)	1860
Jesmond Parish Church (Jesmond, Newcastle)	1858–61
Lambton Castle	1857–62
The Portico (Central Railway Station, Newcastle)	1863

Addenda:

Bolton Hall (West Bolton, Alnwick)	early 19th c.
Mill Race House (formerly the Vicarage, Netherwitton, Morpeth)	date unknown

PERIOD I
1811–1817

The Scottish Presbyterian Church, Howard Streeet, North Shields

The Scottish Presbyterian Church   *(Howard Street, North Shields)*

The Church, now a Salvation Army Hall, has been variously described as 'unsophisticated', 'bold', 'naive' and 'crude' in both its design and its appearance.

The date of the construction is generally believed to be 1811.

The *Newcastle Courant*, of August the 3rd, 1811, supports the claim that John Dobson did indeed build the church in that year.

Newbrough Hall, Hexham, Northumberland

Newbrough Hall *(Hexham, Northumberland)*

A two-storeyed, five-bay, stone house with central pediment and arched doorway, built in 1812 for the Reverend Henry Wastell, by John Dobson.

John Hodgson (*History of Northumberland*, 1820–58) wrote: 'In the year following (i.e. 1812) Mr Wastell built the mansion-house here, in which he at present resides...' [Photographed by kind permission of W. A. Benson Esq.]

The information given to me by the present owner of Newbrough, Mr William Arthur Benson, is that, to his knowledge, the house was built in 1812 for the Reverend Henry Wastell.

The 1992 revised edition of *The Buildings of England: Northumberland*, by Pevsner and Richmond confirm Mr Benson's belief – they, too, are now of the opinion that 1812 is the correct date.

I am also grateful for the following additional information which Mr Benson gave to me, relating to the Hall and its history:

The Reverend Wastell and his wife had two daughters, one of whom died while the other married one of the sons of the Coulson family of Blenkinsopp. William Benson's father married into the Coulson family and he subsequently bought the Hall *c.* 1901.

William was born at Newbrough, in 1905, and has lived his entire life here (he being 92 years old when we had this conversation), except for the time he spent performing military service, rising to the rank of Major.

William's father, on acquiring Newbrough, employed the services of an Edinburgh architect called Deas, who made substantial internal alterations to the Hall and installed the drawing room bay window ... otherwise the outside of the building has not altered from the time it was built.

Linden Hall, Longhorsley, Northumberland.

Rather plain in its appearance the main (west) entrance consisted of a grand porch with four Doric columns.

Linden Hall (Longhorsley, Northumberland)

Charles William Bigge asked his close friend,[1.] Sir Charles Monck, to prepare designs for a large mansion to be built within his estate (on part of the 2900 acres of land he had purchased from the Earl of Carlisle in 1808). It is thought three different designs were prepared before arriving at the final choice.

Monck was an ardent Greek Revivalist and Linden Hall (which Bigge named after the nearby Linden Burn) shows strong examples of this style in the four heavy, unfluted Doric columns of its portico, with its full entablature, frieze of triglyphs and metopes and cornice.

Monck supervised the construction of the Hall from the laying of the foundation stone (on July 30th, 1810) until its completion in 1812 and final occupation in 1813. ('...8th June ... to Linden, where for the first time I slept in my own house.')

It is believed John Dobson collaborated with Monck in the designing of the Hall, after having returned, in 1811, from serving his apprenticeship in London. He was asked by Sir Charles to detail the portico and windows. Indeed, until quite recently it was widely believed that Linden was purely a Dobson house: thus, for example, Pevsner, 1957 edition of *The Buildings of England: Northumberland*, p. 205, who described it as 'an early house by Dobson': and Frank Graham, *The Old Halls, Houses and Inns of Northumberland*, p. 175, who states 'This elegant house, by Dobson, was built in 1812–13, for Charles William Bigge'. However, Mr Bruce Allsopp, *Historic Architecture of Northumberland and Newcastle upon Tyne*,

Linden Hall, The Porch

p. 66, has discovered that the house was, in fact, designed by Sir Charles Monck and that John Dobson's contribution, important though it was, was far less than he had previously been given credit for.

Indeed, Lyall Wilkes (*John Dobson, Architect and Landscape Gardener*, p. 9) makes the point '... had the now known date of Linden (1812) been known previously, more hesitation in the attribution to Dobson might have been shown since so important and large a commission would not readily have been given to a young architect in the first year of his practice.'

Linden Hall was built from local stone quarried from Horsley Common, south of Longhorsley, and Monck was credited with having employed some of the finest stonemasons in the country.

In 1903 Linden Hall was purchased by Laurence William Adamson J.P. The Adamson family lived there for sixty years and during that time were looked after by a full complement of staff. During their period of residence, the Hall was maintained as an auxiliary hospital for sick and wounded British soldiers from the First World War – between March, 1916 and April, 1919.

After the death of Miss Muriel Adamson, the Hall and its contents were sold. It was purchased by Mr John M. Liddell, who lived there until 1978, when the entire Linden Estate was purchased by the Newcastle family business, Callers-Pegasus Travel Service Limited.

Linden Hall and its 450 acres have now been restored to recapture the elegance and style of the original (Bigge) Georgian mansion.

It is now a Grade II listed building.

Above: The Hall is dated 1812. The lovely, four-column porch with its striking, unfluted Doric columns forms the main entrance to the Hall on the west front.

The stone used to build the Hall came from Horsley Common, a mile or so south of the church of Longhorsley. [Photographed by kind permission of Julia C. Marshall (Hotel Manager).]

Cheeseburn Grange *(Stamfordham, Northumberland)*

Before the Dissolution, Cheesburn belonged to Hexham Priory. In 1638 it was the seat of Thomas Widdrington Esq., whose son, Sir Thomas, became Recorder of York. He became Lord Keeper in 1647, Speaker to Parliament in 1656, and

Cheeseburn Grange, the chapel (on right) and the north (rear) face of the Grange.

Cheeseburn Grange, Stamfordham, Northumberland

The west front of the building is two storeys high with tripartite windows. The tall, castellated centre bay has a castellated porch. Attached to the house, on the left is the private Roman Catholic chapel added in 1813. John Dobson's work was carried out in 1813 and 1819.

Cheeseburn Grange with modifications by Dobson

In 1813 John Dobson carried out various alterations to the house for Ralph Riddell Esq – the front door was moved from the south to the west front; he altered the windows; he added the tower over the front door and designed the chapel.

Cheeseburn Grange, West Front

Before the Dissolution Cheeseburn belonged to Hexham Priory. In 1638 it was the seat of Thomas Widdington Esq., whose son, Sir Thomas, became Recorder or York; Lord Keeper in 1647; Speaker to Parliament in 1656 and Lord Chief Baron in 1658. From this family Cheeseburn descended, by the female line, to Ralph Riddell.

Photographed by kind permission of Captain and Mrs S. F. Riddell.

Lord Chief Baron in 1658. From this family Cheesburn descended, by the female line, to Ralph Riddell.

The Widdringtons were deeply involved in the Jacobite Rebellion of 1715. One of the family (who owned the Grange before it eventually passed to the Riddells) was Ralph Widdrington. He was imprisoned and under sentence of death at Liverpool, but managed to escape from the gaol with a servant by means of a rope. During the escape, Ralph lost all the fingernails of one hand through his efforts to cling to the rope. However, it seems that at the time, apart from this misfortune, both he and his servant were suffering from some kind of fever. Fortunately both recovered from their illness and Ralph Widdrington lived on for some considerable time and 'was never molested'.

Above: *North Seaton Hall, near Ashington, Northumberland*

North Seaton Hall *(near Ashington, Northumberland)*

Mike Kirkup, in his splendid book *Was there ever Railway Row? A History of North Seaton Colliery and Village*, published by Woodhorn Press, Newbiggin by the Sea, gives the following information about the Hall and its adjoining Watch Tower:

> 'North Seaton Hall, with its adjacent Watch Tower, was built by the famous north-east architect, John Dobson, whose name is commemorated in one of Newcastle's city streets.
>
> It was initially the property of wealthy William Watson, who owned most of the land around North Seaton, in the early 1800s.
>
> It was eventually bought by the Ashington Coal Company and became the residence of Edmund O. Southern, an agent for the company.
>
> By the late 1920s we find the Hall being used 'to train young lads about to emigrate to Australia, Canada and New Zealand in the art of farming.'
>
> The Hall saw service in the Second World War as a billet for soldiers, and several wooden huts were built in the grounds to accommodate prisoners of war. Upon nationalisation, in 1947, the Hall became the property of the National Coal Board. It was soon housing what we would term today "one-parent families" and others whose social behaviour was somewhat unacceptable.
>
> Like most of the area's fine old buildings, North Seaton Hall was allowed to fall into a state of disrepair and was eventually demolished in 1960.'

Postscript: 'When the bulldozers moved in on a derelict North Seaton Hall, they said it was standing in the way of progress. But when the demolition men came back to raze the colliery village to the ground, they tore out the heart of a thriving community.'

I am indebted to Mike Kirkup for giving me his permission to reproduce this article from his book.

'It is not known, beyond doubt, which was Dobson's first building. Mackenzie, in his *History of Newcastle* (1827), states that "the Royal Jubilee School ... was built between 1810–11, from Dobson's designs" and if this is true, then *it* must be Dobson's first building.

It was also listed in the obituary notice in the *Newcastle Daily Journal* of January 9th, 1865 but it is not listed in Margaret Jane Dobson's list of her father's buildings (in her *Memoir* of 1885), who gives her father's first building as North Seaton Hall, and the date, 1813. Margaret Jane's *Memoir* is often the subject of criticism: its inaccuracies are said to consist of claiming work for her father that was not his. It is difficult to believe (says Wilkes) that John Dobson did not tell his daughter, with pride, which was his first building, so if it *was* the Royal Jubilee School why is it not on her list?'

(Ref. *John Dobson, Architect and Landscape Gardener*, Lyall Wilkes).

Photograph included by kind permission of Wansbeck District Council.

Bradley Hall *(near Wylam, Northumberland)*

The house was built by James Paine in 1750 for John Simpson, a Newcastle merchant, though an earlier property had occupied the site.

The south front has seven bays; the three central bays are under an open pediment and three of the windows in the central (projecting) section are pedimented. The doorway has a Tuscan surround.

Inside, two rooms have fine rococo stucco ceilings and there is a staircase with a delightful Chippendale fretwork balustrade. Mrs Simpson assures me it is the only one of its kind in the entire country.

Bradley Hall, near Wylam, Northumberland

Bradley Hall with entrance moved to east side

Bradley Hall: south and west fronts

Fallodon Hall

Around the year 1813 John Dobson moved the entrance to the east side of the house.

In the *Newcastle Daily Journal* of January 16th, 1865, we read that *c.* 1813 John Dobson made alterations to Lord Ravensworth's mid-18th c. house.

Photographed by kind permission of Mr and Mrs R. M. C. Simpson.

Fallodon Hall *(Christon Bank, Embleton, Northumberland)*

Below: The Hall is basically of red brick. The west elevation has seven bays and sandstone quoins. The centrepiece (which also has quoins) projects and has a recessed arched doorway.

'In Cromwellian times (i.e. mid-17th c.) a Puritan merchant from Berwick, named Sakeld, built a small country house at Fallodon. In the year of Blenheim (1704) Thomas Wood bought the Fallodon estate and shortly afterwards he pulled down Sakeld's house and began building the red-brick mansion, with stone facings, which stood, well-loved by many successive occupants, until it was destroyed by fire in May, 1917. After the "return of peace", Viscount Grey erected the present building on the same site.'

Fallodon Hall, Christon Bank, Embleton, Northumberland

Fallodon Hall. 'Dobson's' east wing

Fallodon Hall.
The east wing (on the right of the photograph) is of dressed sandstone.
The present owner, however, is at a loss to understand why John Dobson did not build the east wing of red brick, in keeping with the rest of the house.

(Ref. G. M. Trevelyan, *Grey of Fallodon*, a biography of Sir Edward Grey, later Viscount Grey of Fallodon.

Trevelyan also tells us that after the fire of 1917 '... only the furniture, pictures and books, on the ground floor, were saved.

After living in the kitchen wing until the war was over, he [Grey] rebuilt the house with the old bricks and in the same general style as before, but with two storeys instead of three and with some changes in the ground plan of the rooms.'

Frank Graham tells that Thomas Wood paid £3,450 for the estate and that he lived at Fallodon for fifty years.

Dobson worked at the Hall in 1815.

Photographed by kind permission of Mr Peter O. R. Bridgeman.

Period I: 1811–1817

Unthank Hall, Haltwhistle, Northumberland.
In 1815 John Dobson made alterations to the Hall for Robert Pearson. Dobson's work is believed to be in that part of the Hall on the left of the photograph.

Unthank Hall, East wing.
The east end of the Hall, where Dobson is reported to have carried out his alterations in 1815 and 1860/62. (Photographed by kind permission of Mr and Mrs W. R. Webster.)

Unthank Hall *(Haltwhistle, Northumberland)*

Nicholas Ridley, Bishop of London, who was burned at the stake in front of Balliol College, Oxford, on the 16th of October, 1555, is reputed to have lived here – though neighbouring Willimoteswick (another Ridley property) would dispute this honour.

Ridley's sister was living at Unthank when he was martyred and this, primarily, has given cause to the belief that Unthank was the Bishop's birthplace.

Prestwick Lodge *(Prestwick Village, near Ponteland)*

A simple, late Georgian, three-bay house of 1815, by Dobson. Described by Wilkes as 'a little gem of a three-bay villa.'

> 'Dobson's best early work, houses such as Prestwick Lodge ... of 1815, are simple and straightforward, late Georgian houses, often with nothing more than a Tuscan or Doric porch, for external emphasis, and a few classical details inside.'

(Ref. *The Tyneside Classical Tradition*: page 17).

Though small by comparison with others designed by Dobson, Prestwick Lodge is considered to be among the very best of Dobson's early houses.

Prestwick Lodge, Prestwick Village, near Ponteland
The 'bath-house' is on the extreme right of the picture.

Prestwick Lodge.
The main entrance doorway with its broad Tuscan pilasters.

Since Mike and Kim Wilson bought the Hall, in 1979, they have carried out an on-going programme of restoration. The original main entrance door (Dobson's) was of soft wood: they have faithfully reproduced and replaced this in hardwood.

In all other respects the doorway is original.

Lancelot 'Capability' Brown (1715–83: renowned Northumbrian landscape gardener) believed that in a garden which was protected from the north and east winds a man might grow 'almost anything'.

Right: *Prestwick Lodge, the stone built bath house.*

Below: *Prestwick Lodge, Garden wall designed by Dobson. This superb garden wall at Prestwick, designed by John Dobson, has a form of boiler heating arrangement at either end of the wall, from which warm air is induced, through ducts, between the outer skins of the wall. Every so often, along the wall, there is a chimney outlet.*

Photographed by kind permission of Mr and Mrs Michael Wilson.

Backworth Hall, Backworth, Northumberland

Backworth Hall *(Backworth, Northumberland)*

Backworth has been a Miners' Welfare Hall since 1937.

The present Backworth Hall (by William Newton, 1778–80) stands on the site of the old Hall of 1675, 'which was small and inconvenient'.

Records show it cost £2,706 to build the Hall with an extra £889 for the wings. The architect's fee was £100.

Ralph William Grey lived here from 1746 until 1812 and it flourished as home to the Grey family until 1822, when years of dispute over the rights to work coal in the Backworth area led to the whole Grey estate being sold to the Duke of Northumberland for £160,000.

Frank Graham (*The Old Halls, Houses and Inns of Northumberland*, p. 21) suggests there is evidence (from the inscription on an old sun-dial) that the Greys were living in Backworth before 1675.

Ralph Grey bought land in Backworth in 1628 and lived till 1666.

The Newcastle Daily Journal of January 16th, 1865, records that in 1815, John Dobson made alterations to Newton's late 18th c. house for R. Greg.

Minsteracres Monastery, Kiln Pit Hill, near Consett, Durham

*Minsteracres Monastery, The north front.
Photographed by kind permission of Father Aelred Smith.*

Minsteracres Monastery (Kiln Pit Hill, near Consett, Co. Durham)

John Dobson made large additions to the Hall for George Silvertop in 1816.

37

West Jesmond Towers, Jesmond Road, Newcastle upon Tyne

West Jesmond Towers, Jesmond Road, Newcastle upon Tyne

(West) Jesmond Towers *(Jesmond Road, Newcastle upon Tyne)*

In her *Memoir* of 1885 (p. 83) M. J. Dobson says her father made Gothic additions to the house of 1817 for Richard Burdon Sanderson from 1823–7 (p. 83).

The Newcastle Daily Journal (January 16th, 1865) reported that John Dobson designed a Gothic villa for Sir Thomas Burdon in 1817. Further alterations and additions were made by both Thomas Oliver, in 1865, and by T. R. Spence, in the 1880s.

A Gothic house, built originally in 1817 and added to from 1823–27 by John Dobson for Richard Burdon Sanderson.

Bought in 1870 by Lord Armstrong's partner, Charles Mitchell. It is now a Roman Catholic Convent High School – La Sagesse.

Photographed by kind permission of the Headteacher, Miss Linda Clark.

Period I: 1811–1817

St Nicholas' Cathedral *(Newcastle upon Tyne)*

In 1817 John Dobson installed a system of heating by stoves in the Cathedral.

Nazareth House, Sandyford Road, Newcastle upon Tyne

Nazareth House (*Sandyford Road, Newcastle upon Tyne*)

Described as a 'simple and straightforward, late Georgian house ... one of John Dobson's best early works.'

Photographed by kind permission of the Poor Sisters of Nazareth and Mr Mark McKelvey of Lamb & Edge (Chartered Surveyors).

Tynemouth Castle

Part of the 'modern' fortifications of Tynemouth Castle – claimed by M.J. Dobson (page 128 of her *Memoir* of 1885) to have been designed by her father, in 1817.

The history of Tynemouth Castle is closely bound up with that of the Priory.

Tynemouth Castle

A site so naturally strong and commanding has always attracted the military-minded.

It is likely that the Romans built a fort here. Since Saxon times a church and fortification have stood on the site. The Norman, Robert de Mowbray, unsuccessfully defied his King, William Rufus, here, and remains of a Norman motte-and-bailey castle lie under the Elizabethan earthworks to the south of the Gatehouse.

The castle stands on a rocky headland with the sea on three sides, north, east and south. The west is defended by the castle proper, which has many Elizabethan military works in front of it.

Licence to crenellate was granted in 1296 and it was then that the headland was encircled with walls and towers.

Like Bothal and Dunstanburgh, Tynemouth Castle is of the 'Gatehouse' type; that at Alnwick was probably copied from it.

To the south the remains of a gallery and solid 13th c. tower still stand, but most of the south wall was destroyed in 1851. Much of the north and east walls have also fallen into the sea.

M. J. Dobson, in her *Memoir* (p. 128), claims that her father designed/built the Castle's fortifications in 1817.

Sources for the above information are Robert Hugill's *Castles and Peles of the English Border*, Brian Long's *Castles of Northumberland*, and Pevsner's *Buildings of England: Northumberland*.

Axwell Park *(near Blaydon, County Durham)*

Axwell Park is an unusually large Palladian Villa, built by James Paine in 1758.

The south front (featured below) has nine bays: the projecting three, in the centrepiece, lie under an open pediment enclosed in which is a coat-of-arms, supported on three corbels. The south front also has a large terrace looking out towards the River Tyne.

The 'post-Clavering' alterations (Sir Thomas Clavering was the man for whom the house was built), both inside and out, were carried out by John Dobson in 1817–18. He also built a garden temple.

Axwell Park
The east front presents a different, though equally interesting, façade. The centrepiece has three bays under the open pediment, enclosing an identical coat-of-arms supported on three corbels. But on either side of the centre is a single, wide (arched) bay containing a recessed, arched window. The east front has been described as 'more villa-like.'

Axwell Park, near Blaydon, County Durham

PERIOD II
1818–20

Doxford Hall, Chathill, Northumberland.

Doxford Hall *(Chathill, Northumberland)*

Described as 'the most impressive house of Dobson's early years.'

Doxford Hall, Chathill, south elevation.
The main (south elevation) has five bays and a Greek Doric porch with fluted columns.

Doxford Hall, external stair.
'... the charming little external stair, in the angle of the north and east wings.'

Photographed by kind permission of Mr and Mrs Brian Burnie.

'Doxford Hall – a classical house for William Taylor.'

(Ref. *Newcastle Daily Journal*: January 16th 1865.)
 The Hall is dated 1818

The Church of St John of Beverley, St John Lee, Hexham, Northumberland.

The Church of St John of Beverley *(St John Lee, near Hexham, Northumberland)*

'A church has stood on or near this spot since the 7th c. when St John of Beverley, while still a monk at Hexham Abbey, came here frequently to pray and on one occasion healed a dumb boy.'

(Ref. Bede's *A History of the English Church and People*: Penguin, p. 271–2)

Tomlinson describes the church as 'a small, ancient structure, with an elegant spire standing …'

T. H. Rowland and Pevsner and Richmond agree that Dobson rebuilt the church in 1818 – 'on the site of a medieval church'.

Wallington Hall, Cambo, Northumberland.
The west front – with its ten bays and projecting wings

Wallington Hall (Cambo, Northumberland)

The *Newcastle Daily Journal* of January 16th, 1865, makes two references to John Dobson's work at Wallington.

The first says he made large additions to the Museum (?) for John Trevelyan in 1818.

The second refers to his later alterations to the 'central hall', in the courtyard of the 17th c. and 18th c. house, for Sir Walter Trevelyan (1853–4).

Wallington Hall, Clock Tower

'Opposite the house stands the Clock Tower, with its handsome cupola and doors spacious enough for coaches or for motors, according to the changing ages. An old plan is evidence that the Clock Tower was first designed for Sir Walter (Trevelyan) as a chapel; but he seems to have thought better of having a chaplain in such close proximity to his privacy ... and therefore preferred the secular version of the building.'

(Ref. **Wallington**, *p. 21: a Privately Printed edition (in 1950) by Sir Charles Trevelyan, Bart.)*
Photographed by kind permission of the National Trust.

Belford Hall *(Northumberland)*

Abraham Dixon bought the village of Belford in 1726 for £12,000. The farming was backward and the 'town' had improved little since 1636, when it was described as 'the most miserable, beggarly, sodden town, or town of sodes, that ever was made in an afternoon of loam and sticks.

'In all the town not a loaf of bread, nor a quart of beer, nor a lock of hay, nor a peck of oats and little shelter for horse or man.'

Dixon's father had been a Newcastle master mariner, of Newcastle Trinity House, in 1673.

Abraham Dixon himself was a successful merchant but hoped his son might do better and become a 'country gentleman', which possibly accounts for his buying Belford.

Abraham Junior succeeded his father in 1743 but gave up trade to devote time to improving his estate, which he did very successfully, planting hedges and plantations, digging ditches, establishing farms and so on.

But more than this, he built a tannery and a woollen factory; he mined coal and built an inn, with accommodation for travellers.

Had he lived today, Abraham Dixon would most certainly have been described as an 'entrepreneur'.

Dixon left the old manor house and in its place he built a new house to designs by James Paine, which was completed in 1756. Three years later he was made High Sheriff of Northumberland – his father's aspirations for Abraham Junior had been realised to the full!

The main façade to the Hall (facing south) is five bays wide and has a 'piano nobile' (i.e. a main floor with a ground floor or basement underneath and a lesser storey overhead).

The central Ionic portico, with four half-columns, is flanked by slightly recessed Ionic pilasters. The entablature then breaks back over the outside windows, only to be brought forward again by twin Ionic pilasters which frame the façade. The side elevations are much simplified versions of the front with the architectural detail reduced to a skeleton. The slight projection of the portico is retained but the pilasters, entablature and pediment have gone and so have the balusters (i.e. 'a bellied pillar or pedestal').

The first recorded visitor to Belford was John Adam, a fellow architect whose rivalry led him to see little of merit in Paine's design.

He visited Belford in March, 1759, and dismisses the main façade as being in poor taste, and the interior as little better. He dismissed the plaster-work (each of the main rooms having a complete entablature) as 'extremely heavy'. Adam mentions an octagonal Gothic tower with extensive views, set on a rocky outcrop to the east of the house. This still survives but in a ruinous state. Together with a small lake and a Chinese cottage, this formed the original 'pleasure gardens'.

Belford Hall, Northumberland

The present park to the front of the house was created in the nineteenth century.

Abraham Dixon died in 1782 and left Belford to his great-nephew, Arthur Onslow (later Lord Onslow), who subsequently sold it, in 1810, to another Newcastle merchant, William Clark, who called in John Dobson to re-order the house. In his inaugural address to the Northern Architectural Association, Dobson condemned the way Paine opened the front door directly into the hall, thus ensuring the house was always cold, together with his practice of placing the hall in the middle of the south front, taking up the best view.

What John Dobson actually said was:

> 'Mr Payne (!) designed Belford House ... In his designs he actually made the entrance of his mansions at the South, entering direct into a hall and from thence to a staircase, providing no check to the rush of air from the main door.
>
> Payne, therefore, effected little or no improvement on his predecessor in the interior temperature of houses.
>
> Moreover, by making his entrance on the side where the best aspect is usually obtained, he prevented the ground from being properly planted, so as to afford the necessary shelter, and deprived the building of the advantage of rich and fully dressed ground about the house.
>
> Mr Payne was, unfortunately, considered a great authority and consequently all the houses built in the north of England were mere copies of Mr Payne's general plan ...
>
> We thus see how much mischief an incompetent man may do, if he be but favoured by fortune and fashion: not only do his patrons suffer but an example is set by which mischief is perpetuated.'

Belford Hall, showing the two wings added by Dobson

For information on Belford Hall I am particularly indebted to Giles Worsley and his article in a reprint of *Country Life* (28th January, 1988), obtained from Belford Information Centre.

(This extract is taken from 'The Address to the Members of the Northern Architectural Association, by John Dobson Esq., F.I.B.A., President. Read at the First Quarterly Meeting, Held April 19th, 1859.')

(Ref. *John Dobson, Architect and Landscape Gardener*, Lyall Wilkes: pp. 105/6).

Belford Hall was built in 1756 for Abraham Dixon, from designs in the classical style by James Paine, who employed the brothers Matthew and Thomas Mills (builders) who, in 1765, were in charge of rebuilding Alnwick Castle. The Hall was enlarged in 1818 by John Dobson for the new owner, William Clark. Dobson added the two wings and altered the orientation of the Hall.

After purchasing the estate in 1810, William Clark called in John Dobson to 're-order' the house.

Dobson condemned James Paine for the manner in which the front door opened directly into the hall, thus ensuring the house was always cold, together with Paine's habit of placing the hall in the middle of the south front, taking up the best view.

In 1818, and to overcome this situation, Dobson turned Belford 'back to front', making a new entrance on the north side, with an Ionic porch opening into a top-lit, single-storey hall.

This then led into the staircase hall.

Belford Hall, Dobson's new entrance on the north side

Dobson also remodelled Paine's three-sided staircase as well as adding large wings on either side of the house.

On the south side these were kept very simple, with detail taken from Paine, but the composition of the north front was deliberately picturesque.

A large, stone mansion, designed by James Paine, and altered and enlarged by John Dobson in 1871–18. Photographed by kind permission of Belford Hall Management Co Ltd.

Belford Hall, additional view

Gosforth Park *(Newcastle upon Tyne)*

According to the *Newcastle Daily Journal* of January 16th, 1865, John Dobson designed the entrance gates to Gosforth Park for Ralph Brandling in 1818.

Pevsner and Richmond believe the date for the gates is 1830.

Gosforth Park, Newcastle upon Tyne

Period II 1818–20

St Nicholas Church, South Gosforth, Newcastle upon Tyne

St Nicholas' Church *(South Gosforth, Newcastle upon Tyne)*

Above: The Church of St Nicholas is a plain structure with an octagonal spire rising from a square tower.

It was rebuilt and enlarged between 1799 and 1820. The architect of St Nicholas' Church was John Dodds. The present church is believed to have replaced a Saxon building.

Rock Hall

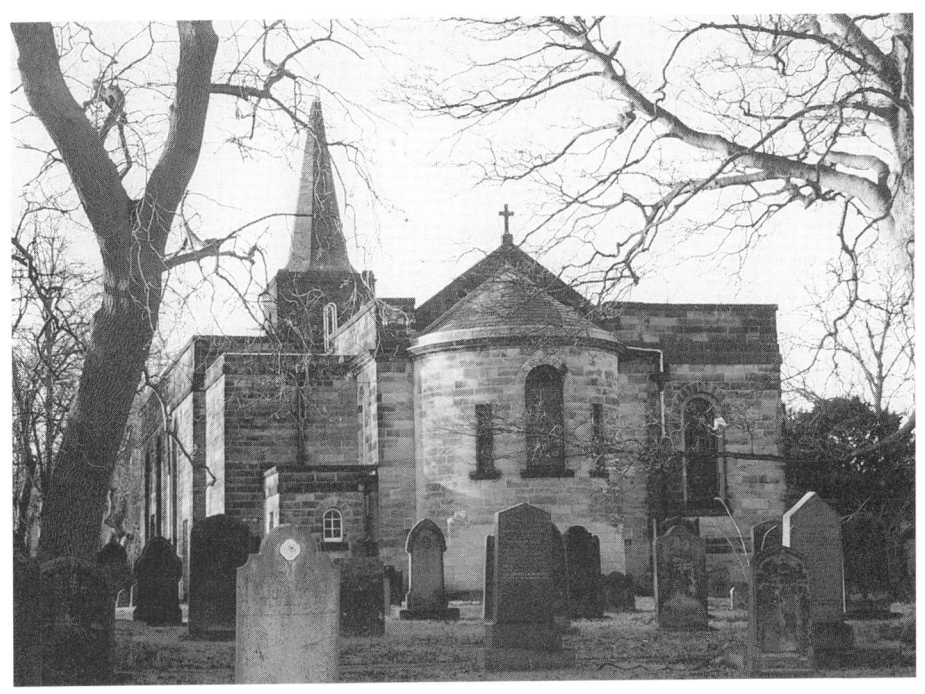

St Nicholas Church, showing additions by Dobson
In 1819 John Dobson added galleried north and south aisles. The south tower porch was added in 1833. The enlargement follows the same classical Georgian lines.

Rock Hall (Rock, Alnwick, Northumberland)

The east front of the Hall, with its crenellated wings and mullioned windows, was burned down on May 15th, 1752. It remained in ruins until 1819, when it was restored by John Dobson for Charles Bosanquet.

Rock Hall, showing additions by Dobson In 1819 John Dobson added the two battlemented, octagonal wings (two storeys high) to the existing pele tower.

Rock Hall, Alnwick, Northumberland

The Bosanquet family believe the pele was founded in the reign of King Stephen, at the beginning of the twelfth century, and was both altered and enlarged during the reign of the first Queen Elizabeth.

The west frontage.
Photographed by kind permission of Mr C. J. Bosanquet.

Hebburn Hall, Canning Street, Hebburn, Co. Durham

Hebburn Hall *(Canning Street, Hebburn, Co. Durham)*

A large 17th c. house – nine bays with a three bay pedimented projection. In addition, the principal windows also have pediments.

In 1819 John Dobson made alterations for Cuthbert Ellison.

Photographed by kind permission of R S Carr-Ellison Esq, of Hedgeley Hall, Powburn, Northumberland: and Ellison Hall Masonic Club (Mr Tony Appleton, Secretary).

Hexham House *(Hexham, Northumberland)*

This is originally an 18th c. Georgian building.

Hexham House, Hexham, Northumberland

Period II 1818–20

Three storeys with five bays and a parapet. It has a porch with square pillars and quoins. The building on the right, masked in foliage, is a nineteenth-century addition.

Photographed by kind permission of Tynedale Council (Mr Alan Batey, Chief Executive).

M. J. Dobson, in her *Memoir* (1885), claims her father made alterations to Hexham House, for T. R. Beaumont Esq, in 1819.

Chipchase Castle *(Wark-on-Tyne, Northumberland)*

Described by Tomlinson as 'one of the most stately and picturesque of Northumbrian mansions.'

There was once a small village of Chipchase, said to date back to Saxon times. A small fort was even raised for its protection by the Umfravilles, who were Lords of Prudhoe, and to whom the manor belonged.

The village continued to be inhabited until the end of the 19th c. Neither it nor the fort exist any longer. In the 13th c. the Pele Tower (described thus by the Reverend C. H. Hartshorne, in his *Feudal and Military Antiquities of Northumberland and the Scottish Borders*: 'The Pele, properly so-called, is a massive and lofty building, as large as some Norman Keeps.' Anyone who has visited Chipchase Castle and seen the formidable Pele Tower would certainly not dispute the judgement of this worthy clerical gentleman. It is believed to have been built by one of the Umfravilles.

In 1348 the manor passed (by marriage) into the Heron family, to whom it then belonged for some three centuries.

Chipchase Castle, Wark-on-Tyne, Northumberland

Chipchase Castle with sash windows added

The manor house was added to the Pele Tower (or Keep) in the reign of James I, by Cuthbert Heron, whose initials and the date, 1621, are cut in stone above the south entrance.

The porch, in the centre of the south front, forms the imposing entrance to the castle.

Legend had it that 'when the heron should be seen charging through a fence instead of flying over it, the extinction of the family was near at hand'. In fact, the last of the Herons to occupy the castle was Sir Harry, who sold both the castle and the estate around the end of the 17th c.

P. Anderson Graham informs us that in times of great danger the cattle were sheltered for safety in a vaulted ground floor room. Above this was the guard-room and, on the third floor, above the guard-room, were the quarters where the family took sanctuary.

Opposite page bottom, above and next page: Dobson's work at Chipchase seems to have been confined largely (even solely) to windows replacement.

The windows between the three arms of the E-shaped frontage were replaced, in 1819, by mullions and transoms.

Many fine houses were improved in the 18th c. by the replacement of sash-windows. In 1784, both the 14th c. tower and the adjoining Jacobean house were given such windows.

The *Newcastle Daily Journal* of January the 16th, 1865, reads '... Chipchase Castle: [John Dobson made] alterations, including some refenestration, to the 17th c. building for John Reed, 1819.'

Chipchase Castle with Pele (Tower)

The Castle is really two buildings: the 14th c. pele (tower) and the manor house, built by Cuthbert Heron in 1621.

The tower is said to be one of the most imposing and best preserved in Northumberland, while the manor house has been described as the finest example of the architecture of its time in Northumberland.

The manor house is crenellated; the 14th c. tower is not, but it has three tiers of Georgian windows to match those of the manor house. The tower's 'crowning motif' consists of four circular corbelled-out bartizans.

Chipchase Castle, the west front.
Photographed by kind permission of Mrs P.J. Torday.

The Hermitage, Hexham, Northumberland

The Hermitage   *(Hexham, Northumberland)*

John Dobson made alterations to the Hermitage, Hexham, residence of R. L. Allgood, in 1819. (Ref. Lyall Wilkes' *John Dobson, Architect and Landscape Gardener*, p. 114).

Michael Cotesworth, who owned the house from 1741–54, rebuilt the south front (of white free-stone and hewn-work), and most of the building dates from this period.

Two-storeyed, with seven bays, the central three-bay section has an open

The Hermitage, south front

The Hermitage, showing the strangely-shaped 'wing' and the neat gardens to the east of the house. Photographed by kind permission of L. G. Allgood Esq., Nunwick, Simonburn.

pediment and pedimented windows. The house also has a hipped roof and balustrade.

The Hermitage came into the possession of the Allgood family through marriage and has remained there for the last two hundred years.

The Hermitage, south front showing balustrades

The Old Rectory (vicarage), North Road, Ponteland, Northumberland

The Old Rectory (Vicarage) *(North Road, Ponteland, Northumberland)*

The *Newcastle Daily Journal* of January 16th, 1865, claims that, c.1820 John Dobson made alterations to the Vicarage. Photographed by kind permission of Mr Philip G. Walton.

The Navigational Beacons *(Guile Point, Ross Sands)*

Following Pages: On a promontory called Guile Point, at the northern extremity of Ross Sands (on the north Northumberland coast), south of, and immediately opposite, the harbour of the island of Lindisfarne, there stand two tall, slender, tapering 'pyramids' of red sandstone ashlar. These two obelisks stand in an east/west line and are some 500 feet apart. Photographed by kind permission of the Brethren of Trinity House, Newcastle.

These beacons, brickbuilt and on a sandstone base, were built by John Dobson for Trinity House in 1820. The east beacon (which is 67 feet high) cost £135 to construct: its west neighbour is some 83 feet high and cost £186.

Inside the outer sandstone 'shell' are the original timber beacons, still in surprisingly good condition. Around 1930, however, the west beacon was struck by lightning and its upper timbers are now charred.

The Navigational Beacons, Guile Point, Ross Sands

Newton Villa Farm, Felton, near Morpeth, Northumberland

The beacons (which are 'listed') were last renovated in 1992. I am greatly obliged to Captain Rennison Shipley of Trinity House for the information above, and to the Brethren of Trinity House for their kind permission to publish my photographs of the Navigational Beacons on Ross Sands.

Newton Villa Farm *(Felton, near Morpeth, Northumberland)*

A plain, three-bay villa (the windows recessed) of *c.* 1820. Ashlar: the west front has a pedimented, recessed doorway. The architect is believed to have been John Dobson.

Newton Villa Farm, view to the east

Thirston House, West Thirston, Felton, Morpeth, the south side with the Tuscan porch (and the west façade)

Top: *The sections of the east side of the house, to the right and left of the three bay (central) porch, are clearly of different periods.*

Above: Thirston House, The Tuscan porch.

Top: Two-storeyed, four-bays with a four-(plain) column Tuscan porch. Attributed to John Dobson, c. 1820. Photographed by kind permission of Mr and Mrs Brian Reed.

Thirston House *(West Thirston, Felton, Morpeth)*

c. 1820, by Dobson, for the Newton family. (Ref. *The Statutory List of Buildings of Special Architectural and Historic Interest*).

Blagdon Hall, Seaton Burn, Northumberland. General view

Blagdon Hall (Blagdon, Seaton Burn, Northumberland)

Blagdon Hall was built (by Matthew White, a Newcastle merchant) between 1735–40 and incorporated a little of its 17th c. predecessor.

Blagdon Hall, Seaton Burn, Northumberland, the south front

Further additions were made in 1826 and 1830. This rather plain north wing (partly by John Dobson) was added around 1820.

The south front has two and a half storeys and seven bays. It has a projecting three-bay centrepiece which is pedimented – as are all the first floor windows.

Photographed by kind permission of The Hon. Matthew White Ridley.

South Lodge, Belford Hall *(Belford, Northumberland)*

The Lodge was probably built by Dobson at the time he made his alterations and addition to Belford Hall ... 1817–18.

Photographed by kind permission of Mr Alan Graham; Chairman, Belford Hall Management Co. Ltd

South Lodge, Belford Hall, Belford, Northumberland

PERIOD III
1821–29

*Hawthorn Tower, near Easington, County Durham, aerial view.
The aerial photograph (reproduced by kind permission of Easington District Council) was taken some time in the 1950s; unfortunately there is no record of the exact date.*

Hawthorn Tower, near Easington, County Durham

Hawthorn Tower *(Hawthorn, near Easington, County Durham)*

Built in 1821, for Major Anderson, from designs by John Dobson. Originally 'Hawthorn Hive Cottage', it was remodelled as 'Hawthorn Tower' by Thomas Moore of Sunderland, *c.* 1850.

> 'A castellated and cement-rendered building, in a highly romantic situation near the mouth of the Dene, it had three and four-light-mullioned and hood-moulded windows and was erected by Major Anderson in 1821, to the design of John Dobson.'

(Ref. Neville Whittaker, *The Old Halls and Manor Houses of Durham*, p. 87).

The house was occupied until the 1939–45 War, but soon afterwards it was abandoned and, in time, became ruinous.

In the early 1970s two young lads aged about fourteen or fifteen were climbing on the tower when one fell and was tragically killed. Easington Council then took the decision to demolish the building. Photograph reproduced by kind permission of Easington District Council.

Period III 1821–29

The Prison, Wooler, Northumberland

The Prison *(Wooler, Northumberland)*

The prison, or Court-house, believed to have been designed by John Dobson, in 1823, still stands on the main street of the village.

Flotterton House, Snitter, Thropton, near Rothbury, Northumberland

Flotterton House (Snitter, Thropton, near Rothbury, Northumberland)

'... the property of Christopher Weallands Esq., who resides here in a handsome and convenient mansion house.'

(Ref. *History, Directory and Gazetteer of the Counties of Durham and Northumberland*, vol II, p. 483, Parson and White 1828).

The house is two-storeyed with five bays: the central (three-bay) section of the south front is a 'bow'. The house was built in 1823 by John Dobson. Photographed by kind permission of F. T. Walton Esq.

Flotterton House, the south front

77

Angerton Hall, near Hartburn, Morpeth, Northumberland

Angerton Hall *(near Hartburn, Morpeth, Northumberland)*

The consensus of opinion appears to be that the house John Dobson repaired in the 1820s (possibly 1823) was rebuilt by him in 1842.

Photographed by kind permission of Mr and Mrs T. E. Stephens.

Angerton Hall, south front

John Dobson's House, 49, New Bridge Street, Newcastle upon Tyne

John Dobson's House (49, New Bridge Street, Newcastle upon Tyne)

A three-storeyed, three-bay house 'with a dainty, honey-suckle frieze' and an Ionic portico – 'spoilt' (says Pevsner) 'by nasty alterations.'

The house was built in 1823. John Dobson died here on Sunday, January the 8th, 1865.

John Dobson's House, another view

Period III 1821–29

Acton House, Felton, Northumberland

Acton House   *(Felton, Northumberland)*

Graham tells us that in 1781 Robert Kisle of Weldon bought the estate of West Acton and part of old Felton for the sum of £9,420.

The mansion of North Acton, or Acton House as it was now called, was enlarged. The main part of the house is built of rich, cream stone. The house, which is attributed to William Newton, is a two-storeyed, seven-bayed mansion. The three-bay projecting centrepiece is pedimented, with four giant Ionic pilasters. A flight of stone steps leads up to a central Adam Venetian doorway.

The *Newcastle Daily Journal* of January 16th, 1865 tells us that Dobson made minor alterations to Acton House for Major Robert de Lisle in 1823.

Photographed by kind permission of Mr and Mrs D. Moore.

Sheriff Hill Hall   *(Gateshead Fell, County Durham)*

Prior to its enclosure in 1822, the land south of Gateshead was one of the least attractive locations in the whole of the north-east of England.

In 1809 an Act of Parliament to enclose and apportion the land came to be drafted, which would create the Parish of Gateshead Fell, but, because of incessant wrangling among the allotment holders, it was another thirteen years before it was actually signed and sealed.

Matthew Plummer was a successful businessman and he was one of the most substantial beneficiaries of the 1822 enactment.

Sheriff Hill Hall

'Matthew Plummer was educated at Sowerby School, near Thirsk, and later studied all aspects of agriculture. He pursued his farming interests until a Mr John Graham Clarke of Newcastle, who was pleased with his industry and ability, transferred him to his office. This was in 1785, and so began his successful association with the city.

'He had an astute business mind and a happy attitude for grasping opportunities. He started in business on the Quayside, as a ship insurance broker, where he did well – Plummer formed one half of the partnership of Plummer & Greenwell, ship and insurance brokers, of 39, Quayside, and his residence at that time was 96, Pilgrim Street, Newcastle.

'In due course he became a partner in the Northumberland Flax Mills and the St Lawrence Bottle Works, and held considerable shares in coal-mines. He bought much land and property, which increased his influence in the North. Matthew Plummer was, for thirty-three years, Vice-Consul for the United States of America.

'He is best remembered, however, as Chairman of the Newcastle and Carlisle Railway.'

(Ref. The *Gateshead Post*: March 20th, 1964).

His sizeable stake in the virgin Parish of Gateshead Fell gave Plummer the opportunity (as it had many other successful businessmen) to aspire to the lifestyle of a country gentleman – with the obligatory country house. He decided (or was it his architect's decision?) to build his house on a site on Church Road, and his architect is believed to have been John Dobson.

'The Hall, or "Sheriff Hill House", was built in 1824 (!) by Matthew Plummer, a wealthy businessman in Newcastle, who preferred to live on the south side of the Tyne, when the outskirts of Gateshead were still 'in the country'. He picked for his new home the healthy altitude of Sheriff Hill, and from the stone which abounds in the district built his substantial residence in an ideal setting.'

(Ref. The *Gateshead Post*: March 20th, 1964).

'An Act of Parliament was passed in 1809 for the division of the common called Gateshead Fell: another act was passed that same year for making this district a separate parish or rectory.

'One acre of land was allotted for the site of the church and churchyard. After various delays the foundation stone of the new church was laid by the Reverend John Collinson A.M., Rector of Gateshead, "upon a lofty eminence" called Sour Milk Hill, on May 13th, 1824, and the building was finished and consecrated, on August 30th 1825; it is dedicated to St John.

Sheriff Hill Hall, which stands at a short distance west of the church, is the property and residence of Matthew Plummer Esq. It was built (about six years ago) on the edge of the hill and is "an excellent and commodious mansion".'

(Ref. *An Historical, topographical and descriptive view of the County Palatine of Durham*: pp. 106 & 109, vol. I (1834), Mackenzie and Ross).

The enclosure of Gateshead Fell in 1822, and the completion of the new line of turnpike in 1827 led to rapid increase in the population and greatly added to the value of land, notably in Low Fell.

By 1827 a 'sod cottage' was a rarity and the spoil-heaps from local coal-mines had nearly all been removed.

Substantial stone houses were soon built: Fell House (for Thomas Wilson) and Sheriff Hill Hall (for Matthew Plummer) were two such.

The latter was a stone villa, built *c.* 1828 (by John Dobson). It was a 'block' of fine ashlar

Sherriff Hill Hall, Gateshead Fell, County Durham

with a central porch of two Doric columns, in antis, with conventional sash windows and a heavy parapet.

The *Newcastle Daily Journal* of January 16th, 1865 claims that the Hall was built in 1823 by Dobson, but 1824 seems the more likely.

(Ref. F. W. Manders, *A History of Gateshead*, p. 310 and Peter Meadows and Edward Watson, *Lost Houses of Durham*, p. 33).

Photographs of Mitford Hall (in Northumberland) and Sheriff Hill Hall (Gateshead) show a striking, indeed remarkable, resemblance in both style and appearance.

Both houses were executed in a severe Greek classical style and consisted of the typical 'square block', with one wing – though Mitford is both larger and more elaborate.

Sheriff Hill Hall is ashlar, with a hipped, slate roof. It is two-storeyed with three bays. The doorpiece has two Greek Ionic columns.

The photograph is of Sheriff Hill Hall (above) reproduced by courtesy of Gateshead Central Library.

Matthew Plummer died on Christmas Day, 1856. A little more than a year later, on February 13th, 1857, the house was advertised for sale in the *Gateshead*

Sheriff Hill Hall

Observer. Here details of the property are given which clearly demonstrate that the Hall was a substantial dwelling, with eleven bed- and dressing rooms as well as the usual ground-floor accommodation – dining and drawing rooms, library and study; extensive servants' kitchens and offices, stabling, coach-house, etc: and all standing on some three acres of land.

(The 'outbuildings', which now form 34–36 Church Road, were probably added some years after the completion of the main building; the earliest record of what now forms these two houses is shown on an 1844 map of the area).

In the late 1940s the main block of the Hall became Gateshead High School, which it remained until 1963 when the house and grounds were acquired by a private building firm, whose intention was to convert the hall into flats.

However, in 1964 Gateshead Borough Council 'bought out' the developer at a cost of some £6000. Thereafter the Council remained undecided on the property's future, until finally, at a meeting on the 15th of July, 1967, they instructed the Borough Architect to demolish the Hall.

'Thornleigh', 32, Church Road, Low Fell (the wing of the old house), is all that now remains of the original Sheriff Hill Hall.

There is some dispute on the subject of when the Hall was actually built. One claim states that Sheriff Hill Hall was designed in 1823 (the same year as Mitford Hall), and that 'the main building was probably completed in 1824.' The *Gateshead Post* (of March 20th, 1964) supports this date and in an article referring to the Hall writes ... 'Although it has been standing 140 years, it is in a fine state of preservation and looks much the same as it did when Queen Victoria was but five years old.'

The Queen, it should be noted, was born in 1819!

Peter Meadows and Edward Waterson, in their book, *Lost Houses of Durham*, assert that the Hall was built 'around 1828'.

The List of Buildings of Special Architectural or Historic Interest – Borough of Gateshead (1983), quotes 'early *c.* 19th', but does not specify a date.

F. W. Mandres (*A History of Gateshead*, 1973) mentions the hall but makes no reference to when it may have been built.

Pevsner & Williamson (*The Buildings of England: County Durham*) make no mention whatever of Sheriff Hill Hall.

Tom Faulkner & Andrew Greg (*John Dobson, Newcastle Architect, 1787–1865*), quoting the *Newcastle Daily Journal* of January 16th, 1865, cite the following: 'house for R (!) Plummer, 1823:' (incidentally, 'R' Plummer was Robert, Matthew's son, who, in 1830, married one Mary Spencer of Newcastle).

Mackenzie & Ross, whose *An historical, topographical and descriptive view of the County Palatine of Durham*, was published in 1834, write, 'Sheriff Hill Hall ... the residence of Matthew Plummer ... was built about six years ago' – viz. 1828.

Thornleigh, 32 Church Road, Low Fell, Gateshead

'Thornleigh', 32, Church Road, Low Fell (Gateshead)

Above: All that remains of Sheriff Hill Hall. Photographed by kind permission of Mr and Mrs Duncan Smith.

The Cathedral Church of St Nicholas (Newcastle upon Tyne)

'The east window was filled with stained glass at the expense of Roger Thornton or his family and the south gable window, a little earlier, by members of the families of Colville and Heton.

'If the north gable had a circular window, it was destroyed in 1824 by John Dobson, who also destroyed the east gable thirty years later. If tracery, formerly in the east window, was older than 1820, its date was not early in the perpendicular style, and the Roger Thornton mentioned on its glass might be Thornton Junior and not his famous father.'

(Ref. *A Chronicle History* ... by H. L. Honeyman, *of the Cathedral Church of St Nicholas, Newcastle upon Tyne*, in *Archaeologia Aeliana*, Vol. IX (4th series, 1932), p. 119).

'In March, 1823, a gale blew three vanes off the steeple and demolished the unfortunate north transept gable window, which had already required the support of flying shores from another building, and John Dobson was called in to report. Dobson was a great classic architect of very refined taste who, on the one occasion when he dared to forget the precepts of Sir William Gell, designed a real masterpiece, the old entrance to the gaol in Carliol Square ...

But where Gothic buildings were concerned, Dobson was rather a destroyer himself, for of medieval architecture, he possessed only that little knowledge which is so dangerous when applied to the restoration of an ancient monument.

The transept gable was almost entirely rebuilt during 1824: the small windows which lit the charnel chapel were closed up and the chapel itself only spared by request of the Vicar, the Reverend John Smith.

The bones of the forefathers were cleared out, the brick penthouse was demolished and the crypt divided into two parts, one entered by a segmental arched doorway, from the churchyard, and the other from St George's porch, by a new opening and flight of steps.

The north gable of the little chantry was altered, the west window of the transept restored (but without its unique transom), and a stone chimney terminating in three pots was corbelled out from the west wall of the transept.

The Vicar had stipulated that the new gable window must be a copy of that it replaced, but Dobson thought he knew better and improved not only its details but its proportions.'

(Ref. *A Chronicle History* ... by H. L. Honeyman, A.R.I.B.A, *of the Cathedral Church of St Nicholas, Newcastle upon Tyne,* in *Archaelogia Aeliana,* vol. IX (4th series, 1932): p. 140).

'In 1827 one of the pinnacles of the steeple was observed to "totter" when the bells were rung. On examination it was found that "the lead coverings having been stripped by the wind", the iron cramps inserted in 1795 had rusted and fractured the stonework, while the cement fillings had perished.

'New capper cramps were inserted and Roman cement filling where required ... small pinnacles renewed in mason work, vanes repaired and regilt.'

The work of the repair to the steeple went on slowly while Corporation and church-wardens argued about liability.

The scaffolding erected in 1827 was still standing in 1829 (and in that year the wardens had a case stated for the opinion of J. Chitty, 6, Chancery Lane).

Therein they mention that 'the Belfry windows are now so very much out of repair that it is dangerous to ring the Bells lest the stone Mullions of the Windows, which are in a very decayed and rotten state, should fall down ... '

Incidentally, in 1831 Major George Anderson, a generous benefactor of Newcastle churches, left £500 for a new bell.

He had reason to think kindly of the bells of St Nicholas for they rang merrily to celebrate his return from gaol, where he had been incarcerated for pulling the nose of the Town Clerk, John Clayton.

The tower continued to crack and tilt southwards until it was fully ten inches off the perpendicular.

In 1832 reports were obtained from John Dobson and also from John Green. Dobson proposed to underpin the tower itself at an estimated cost of £1,200, insert binding courses of cube stones from pillar to pillar, and introduce iron tie-rods at several different points in the superstructure, particularly in the tower and south arcade of the nave; the westmost arch seems to have been restored at this time.

Green proposed to erect new western transepts as buttresses to the lower tower and make them the starting points for a complete refacing of the church in the Perpendicular style of Gothic architecture.

Ultimately it was agreed Dobson should be the Corporation's architect and preserve the tower at the joint expense of church and town, and that, to satisfy the clamour for visible buttresses, Green's scheme should then proceed at the church's cost.

During (Dobson's) underpinning several stone coffins were found just under the pavement on the west side of the tower, proving that the churchyard had formerly extended over what is now St Nicholas' Street.

In 1833, the churchwardens (being £1000 in debt for their share of the work on the tower)

Period III 1821–29

... called a public meeting and appealed for funds. There was a quick and generous response ... so that in 1834, the work, which had commenced on the south side, was continued on the north and finally, in 1836, the west window was rebuilt and the tower entrance doorway reconstructed.

Most of Green's work ... was bolder and coarser in detail than Dobson's and their share (John Green and his son, Benjamin) of St Nicholas' is no exception.

(Among other works) ... they demolished the west end of the north aisle and erected a north-west transept, similar to, but much less substantial than, the south-west one; refaced the entire north aisle, in the perpendicular style; rebuilt the little chantry so that its window and parapet would line with those of the aisle; enlarged – perhaps in conjunction with Dobson – the arches from the tower into the western transepts ... (and so on).

Doubtless in time they would have rebuilt the whole church but death removed John Green in 1852 and his son in 1858.

The deaths of the Greens left the way open for the return of John Dobson, now in his seventies but still an incorrigible 'improver'.

He rebuilt the east gable, in 1859, with a single enormous window instead of the two it originally held.

This did not meet with the entire approval of our Society and at the September meeting Dobson gave a not very convincing apologia for his scheme.

Apparently 'the stonework was not in good condition'. The church authorities wished the new gable to be 'Decorated' and the architect took credit for having instead, adhered to the 'Perpendicular' style of the original, if not to its form. In 1863, the author of the *Daily Journal's Guide to Newcastle* wrote, that the tower needed repair, 'it being hazardous to ring a full peal owing to the dilapidated state of the belfry masonwork.

Mr Dobson has prepared a specification for its restoration, the present condition of the beautiful steeple being quite dangerous. It is not uncommon in boisterous weather to see a group anxiously watching the steeple, which they declare may be seen swaying to and fro with the wind.'

But Dobson died in January, 1865, and when, in 1867, the north side of the tower (lacking the buttresses promised in 1832) began to subside, it was Sir George Gilbert Scott R.A. who underpinned it and rebuilt the crown and lantern, restoring them to the vertical so that they are no longer quite in the same line as the tower ...

Between 1872–7 he ... completed the refacing of the clerestories (clerestories?), which may have been begun by Dobson; removed Dobson's chimney turret (and) completed the restoration of the choir ... (etc).'

(Ref. *A Chronicle History* ... by H. L. Honeyman, A.R.I.B.A., *of the Cathedral Church of St Nicholas, Newcastle upon Tyne*, in *Archaelogia Aeliana*, vol. IX (4th series, 1932): pp. 141–45).

> 'The north aisle was apparently four feet thick before the Greens replaced it, in 1834, and if so its thickness was reduced at that date.
>
> Bell's Plan (of St Nicholas Church, Newcastle upon Tyne, surveyed in 1831–32 by John Bell of Gateshead) confirms ... that the Greens also altered the setting out of the buttresses.
>
> Coming to the Queen's Porch, little chantry or west aisle of the north transept, the plan shows that ... evidently an aisle eight feet wide formed part of the early 14th c. transept and all that was done later was a widening of the aisle by moving its west wall three feet farther out, leaving the old north window and buttress untouched.
>
> The present aisle, built in 1834, agrees in width with neither of its predecessors. The internal plan of this aisle, and of the transept, is as reconstructed by Dobson, in 1824, to form a baptistery with vestry alongside.

The Cathedral Church of St Nicholas

The Cathedral Church of St Nicholas, Newcastle upon Tyne

The reconstructed "school gallery" is indicated on the plan, also the stone pillars supporting the organ gallery of 1785, and the pews and the pulpit, as planned in 1785 and altered in 1798. The east end shows the alterations of 1818 and the gable before it was rebuilt by Dobson in 1859.'

(Ref. *John Bell's Plan of St Nicholas' Church, Newcastle upon Tyne*, by H. L. Honeyman, A.R.I.B.A., in *Archaelogia Aeliana*, Vol. X (4th series, 1933): p. 181).

Period III 1821–29

St Nicholas' Cathedral Church   *(Newcastle upon Tyne)*

St Nicholas' became a Cathedral in 1882.

Much of the present exterior belongs to the 15th c. while the interior is largely 14th c. The original building was severely damaged by the Great Fire of 1248. The crown spire was added in 1470. In 1824 John Dobson painstakingly restored the remains of the north transept window and was responsible for ... major underpinning of the tower.

(Ref. *Newcastle upon Tyne: Northern Heritage*: pp. 52 and 53).

Nunnykirk Hall   *(Netherwitton, Morpeth, Northumberland)*

Opposite Top: The original Queen Anne house stands in the centre of the south front. To this Dobson added the lower projecting wings. To the two-and-a-half-storey, five-bay centre he added an open gallery or colonnade, supported by four Ionic columns. The top of the house has a fine honeysuckle frieze. The wings have full-length tripartite windows while those above are only half the size. To the west he rounded off this fascinating façade with a fine bow-window.

Nunnykirk Hall, Netherwitton, Morpeth, Northumberland

Variously described as one of the finest of Dobson's early classical houses, though it was not a new house but an earlier Queen Anne house which John Dobson re-designed in 1825 – refronting the original house and adding projecting wings. The stonework is excellent.

Nunnykirk Hall, south front

Nunnykirk Hall, the beautiful Ionic porte cochère, which forms the entrance to the Hall on the east side. Photographed with kind permission of Mr S. Dalby-Ball (Headmaster).

The Lying-in-Hospital, New Bridge Street, Newcastle upon Tyne

The Lying-in-Hospital (New Bridge Street, Newcastle upon Tyne)

'The Lying-in-Hospital was moved from Rosemary Lane, in 1826, to a new building, planned by John Dobson, at the junction of Croft Street and New Bridge Street. In 1858 it was decided to amalgamate the outdoor charity for poor women lying-in at their own homes with the lying-in-hospital.

Thereafter the combined charities, under the title the "Lying-in-Hospital and Outdoor Charity for Poor Married Women" continued to occupy the New Bridge Street building until it was taken over as a studio by the BBC.'

(Ref. p. 278 of S. Middlebrook's *Newcastle upon Tyne: Its Growth and Achievements*).

'Designed by John Dobson, in 1825: Gothic style': Mackenzie (1827), p. 518. Pevsner describes it as having 'a three-bay front, and modest in scale'. Photographed by kind permission of the Newcastle Building Society.

Shawdon Hall (Glanton, near Alnwick, Northumberland)

Opposite Top: The west front has five bays with a three-bay central pediment.

Built in 1779 for William Hargrave, probably by William Newton, though the style, both inside and out, is influenced by Robert Adam.

Additions and alterations to the Hall were carried out by John Dobson in 1825.

Further alterations were made in 1858 for John Pawson. Photographed by kind permission of Major R. F. Cowan.

Shawdon Hall, Glanton, near Alnwick, Northumberland

The Fish Market *(Sandhill, Newcastle upon Tyne)*

In her *Memoir* (1885), Margaret Jane Dobson tells the following charming story:

'Mr Dobson designed the Fish Market, Sandhill, Newcastle, the business of which was previously carried out in the open air.

The good ladies who presided over the stalls seriously objected to being removed from their old quarters and for some time Mr Dobson received such an impolite reception from them that he was obliged to avoid their presence.

But when bad weather came and they realised the comfort of their new abode, they relented, and a deputation of fair dames arrived at his residence in New Bridge Street with a peace

The Fishmarket, Sandhill, Newcastle upon Tyne

Period III 1821–29

offering of fish for a Christmas dinner.
Ever after that he was their "cannie Mr Dobson".'

Fish Market, etc., Newcastle upon Tyne: classical additions (by Dobson) to the Guildhall, 1823–26 (Mackenzie: 1827: p. 217).

The Old Vicarage (Haltwhistle, Northumberland)

It has been suggested that the 'core' of the building goes back to the seventeenth century at least.

Below: The canted bay-windows, at either end of the south front (probably part of Dobson's alterations), are a noticeable feature.

The *Newcastle Daily Journal* of January 16th, 1865 tells us that in 1826 John Dobson carried out improvements to the Vicarage for the Reverend N. J. Hollingsworth.

Photographed by kind permission of Mr Colin Creighton ('Coldor', Eden's Lawn, Haltwhistle.)

The Old Vicarage, Haltwhistle, Northumberland

(West) Jesmond Towers, Jesmond Road, Newcastle upon Tyne

(West) Jesmond Towers *(Jesmond Road, Newcastle upon Tyne)*

John Dobson is said to have carried out work here for Thomas Burdon in 1817 and again from 1823–27.

(West) Jesmond Towers, south side

(West) Jesmond Towers, the north side, overlooking Jesmond Dene. Much plainer and less 'ornate' than the more impressive south front. Photographed by kind permission of Miss Linda Clark (Headteacher).

Opposite: The south side (of the building) includes Dobson's work of 1823–27. Faulkner and Greg declared that the corner towers and battlements are elaborately decorated and the windows are … richly traceried, which quite clearly they are.

Bellister Castle, Haltwhistle, Northumberland

The tower (or 'pele') was built by John de Blekensope and was described in 1541 as 'a castle and tower ... in measurable good repair.' By 1715, however, it had become 'a ruinous building' and a century later it was described as 'a rude and crumbling mass of ruins.'
John Kirsopp added the modern house, which was remodelled by John Dobson in 1827.
It was occupied until 1975 when it was given to The National Trust. The present occupants have lived there since 1986.

Bellister Castle   (Haltwhistle, Northumberland)

The castle stands on the summit of a large oval 'motte'. It consists of a 15th c. 'pele-tower' and an adjoining early-19th c. castellated house.

Bellister Castle, the south side of the Tower. Photographed by kind permission of The National Trust and the present occupants of the castle, David and Grethe Taylor.

Bellister Castle

Bellister Castle, a 'close-up' of one of 'Mr Dobson's windows'. M. J. Dobson, in her Memoir *of 1885, says additions were made by her father, in 1826.*

The Chantry, Morpeth, Northumberland. Once a thirteenth century church ('All Saints'), overlooking the River Wansbeck; traces of its origins can still be seen.

The Chantry (Morpeth, Northumberland)

The Chantry was founded for its priest to say Mass, pray for all Christian souls and to keep a Grammar School.

Edward VI granted the school a charter in 1552, and it remained in the building until 1846. Thereafter the building has been used for a variety of different purposes, from cholera hospital to mineral water factory. The building was restored (again) in the 1980s and is now (among other things) a Tourist Information Centre, a Northumbria Craft Centre, a Local History Museum and a Bagpipe Museum.

The Chantry, Morpeth, the east front: twin gables with pairs of arched windows, each surmounted by a single, oval window.

The Chantry

The Chantry, Morpeth, Northumberland.

The west front. A pointed arched doorway; two arched windows, the larger above the smaller (and both recessed), and a nineteenth-century bell-cote. Photographed by kind permission of Castle Morpeth Borough Council (Environment and Planning Services) – Mrs D. Goodwill-Evans, Tourism Officer.

Cathedral Church of St Nicholas, Newcastle upon Tyne. 'Dobson's restored steeple'.

Cathedral Church of St Nicholas (Newcastle upon Tyne)

In 1827 John Dobson restored the steeple of Saint Nicholas' (Sykes ii, p. 213).

> 'New copper cramps were inserted and Roman cement filling where required ... small pinnacles renewed in masonwork, vanes repaired and regilt.'

(Ref. H. L. Honeyman, in *Archaelogia Aeliana*, Vol. IX (4th series, 1932): p. 141–2).

Mitford Hall, Mitford, Northumberland

Mitford Hall (Mitford, Northumberland)

In Hodgson's *History of Northumberland* (1820–58), Part 2, Vol. II, he writes:

> 'The new Manor House, the shell of which is in progress in 1828, is a very handsome, square edifice, built from designs by Mr Dobson.
>
> The beautiful white sandstone, of which its outer walls are built, is obtained from a stratum of rock which forms the bed of the Font. Great praise is due to the owner for choosing a stone for his new residence which is not only beautiful but has every appearance of being indestructible to atmospheric agents. The site of the house is well chosen. This is a fertile and most delightful place.'

Frank Graham's description (*The Old Halls, Houses and Inns of Northumberland*, p. 186) is equally flattering:

Mitford Hall, Mitford, Northumberland.
An ashlar, two-storeyed, three-bay villa with Greek Doric porch and balustrade.

Period III 1821–29

Mitford Hall. The Gate Lodge with Tuscan portico. Photographed by kind permission of Mr B. S. Shepherd.

'Mitford is a handsome, square building, rather plain but relying for effect on the quality of the stonework – the beautiful white sandstone was obtained from the River Font.'

John Grundie and Grace McCombie describe it as 'a reprise of Doxford Hall.' Designed by John Dobson in 1823, the house was not completed until 1828.

Longhirst Hall *(Morpeth, Northumberland)*

In *The Buildings of England: Northumberland*, John Grundy and Grace McCombie write the following description of the Hall:

'Longhirst Hall (designed in 1824) broke entirely new ground. For a start it abandoned the Doric order, for the first time, and used the Corinthian instead.
It is not a large house but the entrance front is a splendid design, exciting and theatrical. It has a tightly compressed, full-height, Corinthian portico, with a pediment – the only time Dobson used a pediment on any of his houses.'

The description of the Hall by W. W. Tomlinson (*Comprehensive Guide to Northumberland*) is exact and colourful:

'Longhirst Hall, the seat of the Hon. J. A. Joicey, is a (modern) mansion of fine grained and warm tinted sandstone built from designs by John Dobson. The house is approached by a projecting portico, graced with two beautifully fluted columns, the capitals of which are original compositions of the architect. The Corinthian entablature, which is surmounted by

Longhirst Hall, Morpeth, Northumberland

Longhirst Hall, south side with central bow

Longhirst Hall. Another aspect

a pediment, is continued round the principal building.
   The conservatory is connected with the house by a cloister open to the south.'

'A particularly fine specimen of a classic mansion, by John Dobson': 1824.
Longhirst Hall is not a particularly large house but its design and construction have been described as 'almost faultless': indeed, the house itself has also been described as 'one of Dobson's masterpieces.'

The south side features a large, central bow: the stonework is superb.

> 'Longhirst Hall was built in 1828, from designs by John Dobson. The great Newcastle architect was then doing his finest work in the classical tradition and this villa is one of his masterpieces.'

(Ref. *The Old Halls, Houses and Inns of Northumberland*, p. 175: F. Graham.)

> 'Longhirst Hall is the most melodramatic of all Dobson's houses. What also strikes the visitor to Longhirst is the magnificent veined and worked sandstone; the pillared entrance portico and inside, the elegant staircase with the ironwork decorated with honeysuckle and other Greek motifs: and the domed roof with its glass centrepiece.'

(Ref. *John Dobson, Architect and Landscape Gardener*, Lyall Wilkes)

> 'Externally it is one of Dobson's finest designs with a balance of strong vertical and horizontal forms and with finely jointed stonework in the now well-established Northumbrian tradition.'

(Ref. *The Tyneside Classical Tradition; Classical Architecture in the North-East, c. 1700–1850*: Tyne & Wear County Council Museums)
   Photographed by kind permission of David Williamson, General Manager.

Longhirst Hall. The pillared entrance portico

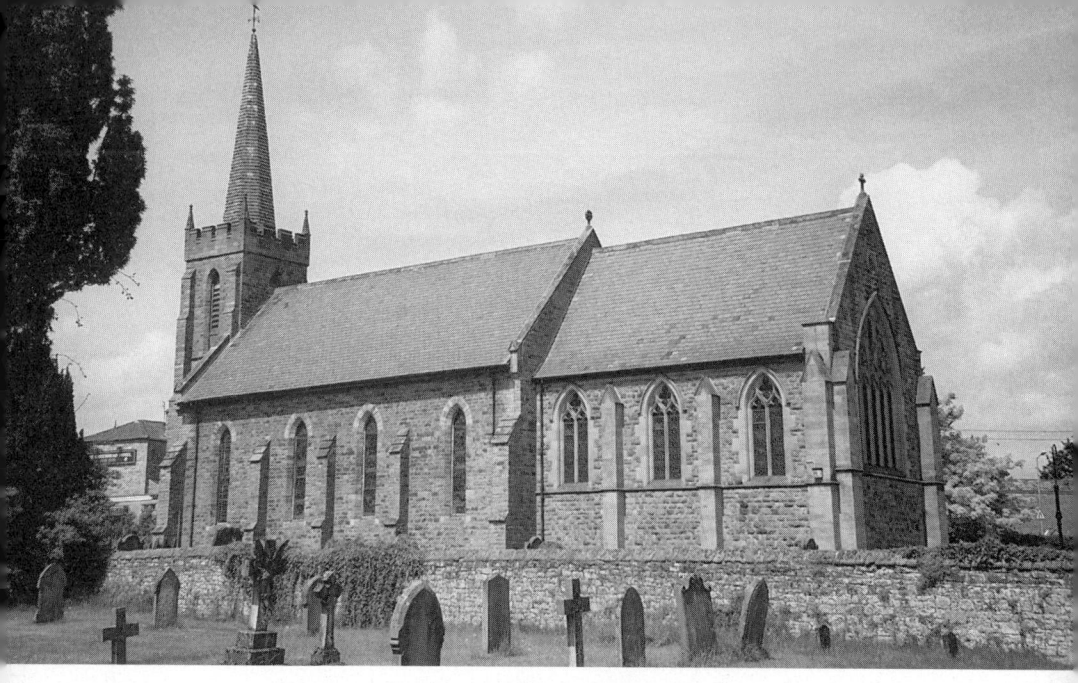

The Church of St Cuthbert, Greenhead, Northumberland

The Church of St Cuthbert (Greenhead, Northumberland)

Designed by John Dobson and built between 1826–28. The design (according to one writer) 'has the simplicity of genuine medieval work.'

The Church of St Cuthbert, Greenhead, Northumberland

High Ford Bridge, Morpeth, Northumberland. The west side, up river

High Ford Bridge   (Morpeth, Northumberland)

High Ford Bridge, on the River Wansbeck, near Morpeth, presents something of a mystery. A notice in both *The Newcastle Courant* and *The Newcastle Chronicle* of April the 5th, 1828 and dated (Mitford) April the 1st, 1828, says that:

> 'At a Meeting of a Portion of the Inhabitants of the Townships of Newminster Abbey and Mitford, held by Appointment at the House of Mr Robert Thompson, Mitford, on the 1st day of April, inst. to consider of some Means of obtaining a better Passage, across the River Wansbeck, at the High Ford, on the Mitford Road, near Morpeth, it was unanimously resolved –
>
> 1. That it is impossible to keep this Ford in a passable State when the Water is the least flooding, owing to the Stepping Stones being placed immediately below the Ford, so as to cause a considerable Wash, making the Ford deep at Low Water.
>
> 2. That it is highly desirable that a Bridge should be erected to remedy this Inconvenience.
>
> 3. That it is the Opinion of this Meeting, a Plan and Estimate having been laid before it by Mr Bryson (who lately erected a Wooden Bridge, across the Tyne, near Haltwhistle, under the direction of Mr Dobson, Architect)

High Ford Bridge, east side, down river

that *a Wooden Bridge* could be erected, ten feet wide and sufficiently strong for the Passage of Horses and Carts and any weight that could be put upon it, for the Sum of £300.

4. That this being the most likely Bridge to be carried into effect, that a Committee of seven Gentlemen *be appointed to collect Subscriptions and to forward the Measure ...

(*The seven Gentlemen of the Committee were:– The Reverend Edward Nicholson; Mr John Moor; Mr Robert Cowl Junior; Mr Robert Thompson; Mr John Anderson; Mr Thomas Blair and Mr Henry Esther).

The Court House

The 'mystery' arises from the fact that just over a year later we find a second notice (dated the 1st of July, 1829) appearing in the issues of *The Newcastle Courant*, on successive Saturdays, July the 4th and July the 11th; and in *The Tyne Mercury* of Tuesday, July the 7th, to the effect that it is now proposed to erect *a stone bridge* across the High Ford!

> 'To the Builders
> To Be Let by Proposal'

> 'The erection of a Stone Bridge across the High Ford, on the River Wansbeck, between Morpeth and Mitford, according to a plan and specification, which may be seen by applying to Mr John Moor, at High House, near Morpeth. The contractors will have to find all materials; also sufficient sureties for the performance of the work, to the satisfaction of the County Bridge Surveyor, with four months from the day of letting.
>
> Proposals will be received by the Committee, at the house of Mr Robert Thompson, in Mitford, on Monday afternoon, the 13th day of July instant, between the hours of three and five, when and where they will attend for the purpose of receiving the same, and of letting the work: in the meantime, any further information may be had by applying to Mr John Moor, as above.' High House, 1st July, 1829.

If ever the wooden bridge was built (which seems very unlikely, bearing in mind the very short time-span between the two proposals) nothing remains of it now.

> 'High Ford Bridge was built by public subscription and under the inspection of the County Surveyor.
> It was begun in 1829 and finished in 1830 and is a handsome structure of two arches.
> The stone for the bridge was brought from Morpeth Quarry.'

(Ref. Frank Graham's 1973 facsimile edition of Rev. John Hodgson's original 1832 publication *A History of Morpeth*: p. 63).

The *Newcastle Courant* of April 6th, 1828, is at odds with Hodgson over the date of the bridge's construction, for it records that 'in 1828 John Dobson built a bridge across the River Wansbeck, at High Ford, on the Mitford Road.'

Opposite: Dobson's bridge (of 1828–30) over the River Wansbeck: east side (down river).

The Court House *(Morpeth, Northumberland)*

> 'Prisoners who had been brought to the bar at Morpeth for trial for felonies committed in this county were imprisoned in Morpeth Castle in the time of Cardinal Wolsey.
>
> The county gaol at Morpeth was originally the private property of the Earl of Carlisle and was rented of him by the sheriff of the county, for the time being, who paid the rent thereof out of his own pocket.
>
> The New Gaol is situated on the south side of the Wansbeck, on the east side of the Great North Road and under banks that overlook it from the south. The act for building it was passed in March, and plans for it, advertised for in June, 1821.
>
> Mr Dobson, architect, Newcastle, was the successful candidate for this great undertaking, which has been completed under his direction at the cost of £71,000. It has been in use as a prison since 1828.

The Court House, Morpeth, Northumberland

    The whole of it has an outline of an octagonal form, stands upon three acres of ground, and consists of an outer wall from twenty to thirty feet high, a gateway, sessions house, chapel, house of correction, wards for debtors and felons, and a governor's house.

    It is in the castellated style of Edward the First and like that of Caernarvon Castle.

    The gateway is an imposing mass of building, seventy-two feet high; and on the ground floor, has in front, on the south, the porter's lodge, and on the north, a grand stone staircase leading to the sessions house; and other apartments above: behind, on the ground floor, are the chapel, on the right as you enter, and the sick wards and bath on the left.

    On the second floor of the gateway, is the sessions house or hall, for county meetings – ninety-two feet by sixty-four feet and forty-one feet high. It is an heptagonal semi-circle, surrounded by a gallery, large enough to hold 3,500 persons, and has under it rooms for the clerk of the peace, counsel and petty jury and cells for prisoners on trial, besides a passage and lobbies for witnesses.

    The ceiling for this and other principal rooms is ribbed and vaulted in a style suited to the character of the exterior of the building ... The governor's house contains apartments for himself and the turnkey, and is in the centre of the gaol area ...

    The debtors' ward occupies the east, north-east and south-east sides of the octagon: the felons' ward is on the south and south-west sides: the gateway on the west and the house of correction on the north-west and north sides. The machinery for pumping the water in the house of correction side is worked by the criminals in the tread-mill manner ...

    The stone for the whole was procured from Morpeth quarry, which lies to the east of the town, on the south side of the river, and has been in use for several centuries.'

    (The masons employed in the building of the gaol were Messrs King, Kyle & Hall).

This information on the Morpeth Court House (the Gaol, as it was formerly) is taken from *A History of Morpeth*, by the Reverend John Hodgson: first published in 1832; this is a facsimile edition, published by Frank Graham, in 1973.

Photographed by kind permission of Chesterton, International Property Consultants, New England House, Ridley Place, Newcastle upon Tyne.

'The Court House is sometimes mistaken for the Castle since it is built in medieval style with battlements and a central entrance. It dates from 1822 and the architect was John Dobson.'

(Ref. *Discovering Northumberland*, p. 58: T. H. Rowland).

'The stately building with castellated towers, at the foot of (the Station Bank) is the County Prison, built in 1821 (!) but now empty in consequence of the prisoners having been moved to Newcastle.'

(Ref. W. W. Tomlinson's *Comprehensive Guide to Northumberland*, p. 244).

'... an imposing, battlemented building, of 1821 (!) called the Court House, which was once part of the County Prison.'

(Ref. *The King's England – Northumberland*, p. 162: Arthur Mee).

'Coming down the avenue of trees from Morpeth Station, the visitor is greatly impressed by the stately building looming up before him. It was the County Prison ... In the 19th c. Morpeth Gaol was a terror to the horsecopers, muggers and other gangrels who were credited with the thefts and burnings which constituted the more ordinary forms of crime in North Northumberland.'

(Ref. *Highways and Byways in Northumberland*, p. 357: P. Anderson Graham).

'In 1821 John Dobson won a competition for the design of the Northumberland Gaol, House of Correction and Sessions House at Morpeth. Built (1822–28), like its Newcastle counterpart, of local stone and equivalent in scale, size and cost, it was more authentically castellated in style – Dobson himself said his design was inspired by the castles he had seen at Conway, Beaumaris and Caernarvon. Morpeth and Newcastle Gaols (were) two of the most important designs of Dobson's whole career.'

(Ref. *John Dobson, Newcastle Architect, 1787–1865*, p. 44, Faulkner & Greg).

St Mary's Parish Church (Belford, Northumberland)

'It isn't known when the first church was built in Belford but there was one in 1100 – probably a wooden building served by the monks of Lindisfarne. The first stone church was built in Norman times, around 1200. In 1615 the church was entirely rebuilt and was a plain, rectangular design with a door at the west end of the south side and a bell turret; the date 1615 is carved over the door nearer the east end.

Due to the poor state of repair, an extensive restoration programme was carried out in 1700.

The restoration of the chancel, by John Dobson, was started in 1828 and in 1829 the present building was built.

As the old building was unable to accommodate the population, the north aisle was added and a gallery above the north and west aisles was constructed. The bell turret was replaced by a tower surmounted by four pinnacles. It is thought that during this rebuilding, the private chapel was incorporated into the church, to become the chancel.

The most interesting feature of the chancel (apart from the Norman arch) is the small south window, which is the one original window left untouched in the building. It has since been filled with glass designed by Harold Easton. The clock was installed in the tower in 1841: the porch was added in 1844 – "great complaints having been made in winter about the cold in that part of the church."'

St Mary's Parish Church, Belford, Northumberland

The porch cannot have been an unqualified success for we are told '... the congregation continued to shiver until 1854, when gas stoves were purchased. The pulpit was replaced in 1860 and the old "box pews" were removed in 1879 and replaced with those we see today.'

(Ref: *Church notes*, printed by How and Blackhall of Marygate, Berwick-upon-

St Mary's Parish Church, Belford, Northumberland, another aspect

Tweed.) Extracts reproduced by kind permission of the Rev. Adrian J. Hughes, Vicar of St Mary's (June, 1998).

In 1829 John Dobson rebuilt the nave and added a north aisle and the west tower.

Lilburn Tower *(Alnwick, Northumberland)*

Designed in 1828, for Henry Collingwood, to replace an earlier house, it is in all respects, 'except its architectural style', a perfect example of an 1820s Dobson house.

Below and next page top: The entrance front would have been perfectly symmetrical had Dobson's design remained unaltered but his plan had to be modified. The porte-cochère was subsequently moved from a position between the projecting wings to the position it occupies now. This was done (some time between 1840–50), we are told, to prevent draughts from outside finding their way into the main hall.

'When the foundation stone of Lilburn Tower was laid, on January 3rd, 1829, (*Country Life* – November 8th, 1973) there was buried in the foundations a manuscript commemorating not only the names of Thomas Wallace and Sons, the Newcastle joiners, who made the dining-room furniture and bookcases from John Dobson's designs, and Ralph Dodds (plasterer), but also Robert Wallace (Clerk of Works) and Robert Hall (the mason from Alnwick).'

Gervase Jackson-Stops, writing in *Country Life* (November 8th, 1973) said 'Dobson's dexterity in translating Greek into Tudor must be admired, for the result is completely successful.'

'The extra cost involved in departing from the straight lines and simplicity of the classical design into the realms of the picturesque is shown by the fact that

Lilburn Tower, Alnwick, Northumberland

Lilburn Tower, Alnwick, Northumberland

Built in the middle of his finest Grecian period, is, in reality, a symmetrical, classic design, wrapped in a Tudor-Gothic veneer. It is a beautiful house, nevertheless; wonderfully sited (as almost all of Dobson's houses were) and with a fine and complete set of his own decorations and furnishings.'

Left: *The magnificent porte-cochère*

Lilburn Tower, further views

Lilburn Tower, West Lodge

the cost of Meldon Park (1832) was £7,188-1-11 (excluding the stables), while the cost of the towers and turrets at Lilburn (in 1828, four years earlier) was £21,975 (also excluding the stables!).'

Writing in Pevsner and Richmond's book, *The Buildings of England: Northumberland*, John Grundy and Grace McCombie make the following observation: 'Dobson was equally happy to design in the Gothic style, though the results are not so unreservedly successful.

His best Gothic buildings are substantial country houses.'

Above: West Lodge. A single-storey Tudor lodge. Photographed by kind permission of Mr Duncan Davidson.

Embleton Old Vicarage (now Embleton Towers) *(Embleton, Northumberland)*

'The most substantial part of the present house dates from 1828 and was designed by John Dobson ... for George Dixwell Grimes, Vicar from 1822–30. Dobson refaced the south-western end of the tower, inserting new windows, and built a large extension with handsome reception rooms overlooking the garden. Best known as a classicist, in this instance Dobson chose to work in a restrained neo-Tudor style, so advanced for its time that the former vicarage is often taken to be Victorian rather than Georgian.

For his new additions Dobson used the local whinstone, hard to work but very durable. Dobson built with a keen understanding of the unsparing northern climate, providing extra insulation of lath and plaster under the main floors and skilfully planning his entrance lobby to intervene between the main entrance hall and the draughts and winds from the front door. In the late 1970s a new vicarage was built (Dobson's house, by then, proving 'inconveniently large in the changed social conditions of the 20th c.') and for the first time, after several centuries, the house passed out of ecclesiastical occupation.'

Embleton Old Vicarage, Embleton, Northumberland

(Ref. R. B. Dawson's *The Story of Embleton*, (1931): H. L. Honeyman's *Embleton Vicarage* – a paper read to the Society of Antiquaries of Newcastle-upon-Tyne, (April 25th, 1928); and Edward Bateson's *A History of Northumberland*, Vol. ii (1895).)

Pevsner and Richmond (*The Buildings of England: Northumberland*, p. 271, the 1992 revised edition) have this to say of the Old Vicarage: 'Often cited as a "vicar's pele", indeed, in Pevsner's 1957 edition of this book he wrote:

> 'Embleton possesses one of the typical Northumbrian "Vicar's peles": it is mentioned in the list of 1415', (p. 148) but the oddly elongated tower, which forms the east wing of the present building, may have begun as a more conventional house ... in the 14th c., before being remodelled as a tower, late in the century.
>
> By the 18th c., if not earlier, the tower was again reduced to being a wing of a larger house. This was largely rebuilt in 1828 by John Dobson in his castellated Tudor style, using local whinstone.
>
> Attached to his west wing is a contemporary conservatory, an elongated octagon, in plan, with a swept hipped roof.
>
> Dobson's interiors are well-preserved with good cornices and Gothic fireplaces; this is one of his smaller houses but among the most attractive.'

In 1928 H. L. Honeyman gave this illuminating description of the 'Vicarage':

> '... larger windows were inserted in the stark walls and an annexe was added south-westward. Later a new wing was built still farther to the south-west. Then the old tower was re-roofed and its interior modernised.

Embleton Towers, the Conservatory

Finally, in the reign of George IV (1820–30), the vicarage became too mean for its vicar; part of the earlier work was removed, part re-faced and a vast new wing, containing nine rooms, a main staircase and a conservatory, was constructed.

'... it is said that when last the charge was vacant a prospective Vicar of Embleton came, saw the vicarage, and immediately departed!'

According to the *Newcastle Daily Journal* of January 16th, John Dobson made substantial Tudor Gothic additions to the pele tower for The Revd. George Dixwell Grimes, in 1828. In that same year he built-on a south-west corner to the vicarage, including drawing room and dining room, in his 'manor house' style.

This information is all corroborated by the present owner of the house, Mr K.J. Seymour-Walker, who also told me the following interesting story: Apparently, in 1832, the clerical incumbent of the time, pleading hardship, applied for 'Queen Anne's Bounty' and was promised a loan of some £700 to carry out alterations.

Embleton Towers, Embleton, Northumberland

John Dobson said that if he pulled down the existing frontage and used the same stone to carry out the work, he could certainly complete the job for the same sum. To this proposal the Vicar was happy to agree.

The conservatory referred to by both Honeyman and Pevsner is believed by the owner of the Towers to be a Dobson creation.

The roof consists of arched, cast-iron ribs (which was Dobson's style) and for this reason (the owner suggests) it could not have been built later than 1845.

Mr Dobson, as we know, was notoriously bad at keeping records of his work and unfortunately there appears to be no actual record of who built the conservatory, but the 'laws of probability' seem to suggest John Dobson.

Frank Graham (*The Old Halls, Houses and Inns of Northumberland*, p. 113) says work on building the pele is uncertain but:

> 'seems to have started in 1332 and was completed in 1341.
> ... around 1828 the house was remodelled and increased considerably in size, after designs by John Dobson.'

Embleton Towers, Embleton, Northumberland, another view

'Late in the Georgian period the brick-built, south-west wing and kitchen were added and the whole building was plastered, or "harled", externally. Some parts of this, together with the present tower roof, were no doubt the work of James Boulter (1811–22), who, after his death, was judged so severely by Archdeacon Singleton, in his visitation of 1828 (who said 'Mr Boulter put a new roof on the house, but never paid for it. The more recent additions have been in pitiful taste, and the rooms are so low as to be hardly wholesome.')

In the time of George Dixwell Grimes (1822–30) some parts of the later additions were taken down, the south-west end of the tower was refaced and a large new wing erected facing the garden, which was also altered and extended. All this work was designed by John Dobson of Newcastle and it is very advanced for its date, so much so that, but for Archdeacon Singleton's evidence, I would have credited Grimes with the back stair wing only, and attributed the extension to George Rook (1830–74), in whose time Dobson built the north transept of Embleton Church and lengthened the nave aisles westward to embrace the church tower ...'

(Ref. H. L. Honeyman A.R.I.B.A., writing in *Archaelogia Aeliana*, Vol. V (4th series, 1928), p. 91).

Photographed by kind permission of Mr K. J. Seymour-Walker.

The Village Cross

The Village Cross, Holy Island

The Village Cross (Holy Island, Northumberland)

The old village of Holy Island is beside the harbour. In the square (formerly the market place), on the green, is a beautiful stone Celtic cross. It stands twelve feet high and was rebuilt by John Dobson, at H. C. Selby's expense, in 1828 – as its inscription reads.

It stands on the pedestal of 'St Cuthbert's Cross', erected by Bishop Aethelwold.

(Ref. The *Newcastle Daily Journal* of January 16th, 1865: *The King's England: Northumberland*; Arthur Mee: and *Comprehensive Guide to Northumberland*; W. W. Tomlinson).

Period III 1821–29

St Mary's Place, Newcastle upon Tyne

St Mary's Place *(Newcastle upon Tyne)*

Built to designs by John Dobson in 1830.

The *Newcastle Chronicle* of 6th June, 1829 and the *Newcastle Courant* of 20th March, 1830 describe St Mary's Place simply as 'a Tudor terrace, from 1829'.

Midland Bank, to its credit, has preserved the original doorway with flight of stone steps flanked by iron railings.

St Mary's Place, details of doorways

Church of St John the Baptist, Grainger Street/Westgate Road, Newcastle

Church of St John the Baptist (Grainger Street/Westgate Road, Newcastle)

In 1829 John Dobson restored the chancel and the gables of the church.

Harbottle Castle (House), Northumberland

Harbottle Castle (House), Northumberland

Harbottle Castle (House)

Harbottle Castle (House) (Northumberland)

Opposite Bottom and Above: Stone from the medieval castle was used to build a fine 17th c. house for the Widdrington family.

Alterations were made, in 1892, by John Dobson for Thomas Clennell.

A rather plain, two-storeyed, five-bay villa, in sandstone ashlar, with a rather unusual porch. Photographed by kind permission of Mr and Mrs J. E. Wilson.

The Hall, Glanton Pyke (Glanton, Alnwick, Northumberland)

It has a two-storeyed, five-bay, ashlar south front, with pedimented doorway.

The *Newcastle Daily Journal* of January 16th, 1865, claims that in 1829, John Dobson made alterations to the house for Henry Collingwood.

The east front also has five bays; the central porch is believed to be a late nineteenth-century addition.

The Hall, Glanton Pyke, Glanton, Alnwick, Northumberland

The Hall, Glanton Pyke, east front

'Glanton Pyke ... used to be the beacon hill, but now a mansion stands on its summit.'

(P. Anderson Graham: *Highways and Byways in Northumbria*). Photographed by kind permission of Mr and Mrs John S. R. Swanson.

The Hall, Glanton Pyke, another view

PERIOD IV
1830–39

The Church of St Andrew, Bywell, n/r Stocksfield, Northumberland

The Church of St Andrew *(Bywell, n/r Stocksfield, Northumberland)*

This church is said to have the finest Saxon tower in the country: the nave and chancel have been much reconstructed since they were first built in the 13th c. Little original work remained – only the 'lepers' squint' and the piscina in the south transept.

The church was altered by John Dobson in 1830 and again, later, in 1850.

St Thomas' Crescent *(Newcastle upon Tyne)*

Allsopp and Clark suggest the Crescent is 'probably by John Dobson', c. 1820–30.

Andrew Greg describes the houses (with their doorways with Doric Pilasters and heavy architraves) as 'standard Newcastle terracing of the first half of the nineteenth century.'

St Thomas' Crescent, Newcastle upon Tyne

Woolsington Hall, Woolsington, n/r Ponteland, Northumberland

Woolsington Hall

(Woolsington, n/r Ponteland, Northumberland)

A number of features of the hall strongly suggest late 17th c. handiwork – possibly that of the architect Robert Trollope.

The centre of the south front is said to be in "the capheaton style", but with timber mullions and transomes on the ground floor windows, and 'ovolo-moulded stone' ones on the floor above.

The wings at either end of the stone frontage, with the white ornaments in each corner, are dated 1794.

On p.85 of her *Memoir*, Margaret Jane Dobson tells us that in 1828 her father, John Dobson, made alterations to Woolsington Hall for Matthew Bell.

Photographed by kind permission of Cameron Hall Developments Ltd.

Church of St Thomas the Martyr, Barras Bridge, Newcastle upon Tyne

Church of St Thomas the Martyr (Barras Bridge, Newcastle upon Tyne)

In 1820 a decision was made to demolish the Chapel of the Bridge of Tyne situated at the north end of the Tyne Bridge, Sandhill (in 1770 the west end had already been demolished and in 1782 it had been further reduced in size). At their own expense, the Corporation of Newcastle decided to erect a new chapel at Barras Bridge on Magdalene Meadow, which belonged to St Mary Magdalene Hospital.

The Act of Parliament for the erection of the new chapel was given the Royal Assent on the 21st of June, 1827.

In July, 1827, plans by the Newcastle architect, John Dobson, were approved by the Corporation to erect a new chapel.

Church of St Thomas the Martyr, Barras Bridge, Newcastle upon Tyne, another view

This would cost some four thousand five hundred pounds and would seat twelve hundred people.

(Ref. *Archealogia Aeliana* (5th edition): volume XI p. 302)

Designed by John Dobson in 1827–30 and consecrated on October 19th, 1830. It was described by one Mr Burn, an Edinburgh architect, to John Clayton, the Town Clerk, as 'one of the most chaste and elegant buildings of the size in the Kingdom.'

(Ref. Mackenzie: Vol. 2, p. 765).

'The slenderness of the structure is remarkable: the balcony was an unfortunate addition.'

(Allsopp and Clark).

Above: *Church of St Thomas the Martyr, Barras Bridge, Newcastle*

Left: *The Church of St Nicholas, West Boldon, County Durham*

Church of St Nicholas (West Boldon, County Durham)

Opposite Bottom: The Newcastle Courant of July 31st, 1830, tells us that, in that year, John Dobson added a gallery to the Church of St Nicholas.

Chollerton Grange, near Hexham, Northumberland

Chollerton Grange *(Chollerton, near Hexham, Northumberland)*

Dr Frank Atkinson is of the opinion that the Vicarage (now the Grange) is early 19th c. and 'of two builds' largely by Dobson, a suggestion seemingly confirmed by Pevsner, who refers to the dates CB/1830 and CB/1847 on different sections of the house.

The owner, however, insists (and he should know) that the work is entirely the work of Dobson. Drawings, coded 1875/C, are to be found in the Northumberland Record Office.

A two-storeyed, hipped-roof building with an open, projecting pediment. It has three bays, though the ground floor window on the left, unlike the others, is tripartite.

John Dobson worked on the Grange both in 1830 and in 1847, for two Vicars of Chollerton who were father and son.

'Lyall Wilkes', declares the owner, 'wrongly assumed that only part of the house was Dobson's work whereas it is, in fact, entirely Dobson's.' Photographed by kind permission of the owner.

Watergate Building, Sandhill, Newcastle upon Tyne

Watergate Building   (Sandhill, Newcastle upon Tyne)

The Watergate Building stands on the site of the Bridge Chapel of St Thomas the Martyr, which was demolished in 1830 'because it obstructed traffic'. The present building, which took its place, was designed by John Dobson.

The Watergate Building, which was designed by John Dobson: facing north and west. Photographed by kind permission of Home Housing Association 1998 Ltd., Regent Centre, Gosforth, Mr Colin Garbutt (Regional Director).

Burnhopeside Hall *(Lanchester, County Durham)*

A small, two-storeyed mansion (of *c.* 1820), three bays wide, 'built on the site of an earlier farm' (the remains of which can still be seen on the right of the main building).

The centre section of the south face projects slightly and the entrance is via a square porch with arched doorway, which may have been added later. Photographed by kind permission of Mrs Christine Hewitt.

Burnhopeside Hall, Lanchester, County Durham

Right: *(14–20) Great North Road, Barras Bridge, Newcastle upon Tyne*

Below: *(14–20) Great North Road, Barras Bridge, Newcastle upon Tyne, another view*

(14–20) **Great North Road** *(Barras Bridge, Newcastle upon Tyne)*

A short terrace of houses (of the early 1830s), on the east side of the Great North Road, has been attributed to John Dobson.

Number 14 has three short, individual balconies. There is a single balcony from 16–18 (inc.) and number 20 has no balcony. The balconies appear to be purely decorative rather than functional, though whether this has always been the case I cannot say. The houses are four-storeyed (including basements). There are two projecting wings, each three bays wide: the remainder of the terrace is slightly recessed and is nine bays wide.

Chesters, Humshaugh, Hexham, Northumberland

Chesters *(Humshaugh, Hexham, Northumberland)*

The house was built in 1771, by John Errington. The architect was John Carr of York. Additions were made by John Dobson in 1832 and 1837.

> 'Alterations were carried out ... in 1832 and 1837 by that most prolific Newcastle architect, John Dobson.'

(Ref. *Archaelogia Aeliana* (4th edition): Vol. XXXVI, p. 223). Photographed by kind permission of Mr George Benson.

Chesters, Humshaugh, Hexham, Northumberland

Meldon Park. The east front is very similar to that at Mitford: three closely spaced windows in the centre but with tripartite window at either end.

Meldon Park   *(Hartburn, near Morpeth, Northumberland)*

John Grundy and Grace McCombie write:

'... the last of the great Greek houses was marked in the design by a return, on a larger scale and with a little more sophistication, to the simple elegance of Mitford.'

Photographed by kind permission of Mr M. J. B. Cookson.

Meldon Park. The south view overlooks the valley of the River Wansbeck.

*Wynyard Park, Billingham, Cleveland. The magnificent pedimented portico.
Photographed by kind permission of Sir John and Lady Hall*

Wynyard Park, Billingham, Cleveland, general view

Wynyard Park (Billingham, Cleveland)

Described by J. M. Robinson as 'probably County Durham's nearest equivalent to a grand stately home.' 'Its design is said to be based on 'unexecuted proposals' for a Waterloo Palace for the Duke of Wellington.

The building took almost nineteen years to complete and cost more than £102,000. In 1841 a fire broke out in the chapel at the west end and, damaging more than two-thirds of the building.

John Dobson was employed to provide additions in 1832 and again after the fire in 1845.

Benwell Tower (Newcastle upon Tyne)

'The imposing castellated building', says Tomlinson, 'stands on the site of an old tower which belonged to the Priors of Tynemouth and was their summer residence. Attached to the tower was a small domestic chapel and a burying ground wherein interments took place, until 1759.'

Rebuilt by John Dobson (1830–31). A square, castellated, Tudor Mansion

Benwell Tower, Newcastle upon Tyne

built on the site of an ancient tower. Photographed by kind permission of the BBC.

The 'New Bridge' (Morpeth, Northumberland)

> 'It consists of three arches – the middle one of 50 feet and the two side ones of 40 feet span; and the breadth of the arches, across their soffits, is 32 feet 6 inches; the largest to rise 16 feet and other two 13 feet each.
>
> The stone for it is all brought by the railway from Netherton and is of excellent quality.'

(Ref. *A History of Morpeth*: the Reverend John Hodgson; 1832).

Debate over the siting of the New Bridge had caused a considerable degree of bitterness, controversy and not a little anger among sections of the people of Morpeth.

Some evidence of this inevitably found its way into the columns of certain newspapers and though only a few of the worthy citizens were prompted and prepared to air their protests publicly, it seems more than likely that a great many more were ready to express their views in the inns and taverns, shops and private residences in the town.

Three townsfolk, at least, committed their thoughts to paper and though making use of a pseudonym, their missives were duly published in the pages of *The Newcastle Courant* and *The Newcastle Chronicle*. Two of the letters have been preserved on page 18 of *Morpeth Collectanea* (1826–39): Vol 3 (N.C.R.O.)

The first letter, dated October the 30th, 1828, and signed 'An Inhabitant of Morpeth', is an 'open letter' addressed to Matthew Bell Esq, M.P. A brief note

The 'New Bridge,' Morpeth, Northumberland

(prefixed with three stars) in the November 1st edition of the *Courant*, says that 'The letter to M. Bell Esq, M.P. came too late for this week.' Nevertheless, the letter, in its entirety, is to be seen in the subsequent copy of the *Courant*, printed on November 8th, on which date it is also to be found in *The Newcastle Chronicle*.

The writer refers to a memorial presented to Matthew Bell on the day he chaired the meeting of the Bridge Committee (October 30th), of which Bell was a member, at the Queen's Head Inn, Morpeth.

The memorial was presented by the Proprietors and Tenants of Houses and Premises situated in the lower part of Bridge Street, asking that their interests might be taken into consideration when the siting of the bridge was decided.

It transpired that a decision had been taken by a majority of the Committee:

> 'That the local Interests of the People of Morpeth should not, on any Account, be consulted on any Matter relating to building of the Bridge.' This, the writer angrily contends, is unjust, unfair, illiberal and unfeeling – and, moreover, 'a complete insult to the people of Morpeth.'

Clearly more than disgruntled, 'An Inhabitant of Morpeth' asserts that if the 'New Bridge' were to be constructed near the old one, the cost would be in the region of £10,000 (in fact, it cost less than half this sum):

> 'but if a new line of road is made ... through the hills and bogs, directly to the Market Place adjoining the Town Hall, £20,000 will be barely sufficient for the purpose.'

'And for what purpose?' he asks. 'What advantages would be gained by this line that would not be obtained by a site lower down the town?'

'Half the people of Morpeth would be ruined in their business', he claims, 'and their property lessened one half in value.'

The writer advises Matthew Bell that the Committee are honour bound to adopt that plan (for the siting of the bridge), 'all things being equal', 'which is the cheapest and least burdensome to the community at large.'

Our correspondent seems convinced that vested interests are at work and names the 'villain of the piece' as one Mr Brandling and his party. He calls the plan 'absurd and silly'.

He concludes that should the people of Morpeth, particularly those whose interests are most in danger, be unable to make the Committee attend to these interests, then the people should take their grievance to Parliament, where, doubtless, 'they will obtain redress.'

The second complainant signs himself 'Publicola'. His letter was published in *The Newcastle Chronicle* on both November 1st and 8th and in *The Newcastle Courant* on November 8th.

He shares the belief that public disquiet should be taken into account but at the same time has harsh words for those parties 'who think their pecuniary interests and convenience are likely to be affected by this useful public work ...'

'Publicola' complaints bitterly that as the bridge is to be a toll-bridge (the Subscribers having their Principal and Interest secured by a public toll), the 'New

Bridge' is, in effect, to be built by the public. Under these circumstances, declares 'Publicola', '... will anyone with a Spark of Public Spirit or Gentlemanly Feeling in his Composition stand forward and contend that the Public Convenience ought not to be the *primary* Consideration?'

However, he renews his attack on those who are 'biased by some petty self-interest' and the 'narrow, selfish, mistaken views of a few interested individuals.'

He also views the threat to petition Parliament as 'the mere vapouring of selfishness in despair' and 'utterly ridiculous.'

Our anonymous correspondent concludes his letter by expressing the opinion that three quarters of the town's population would benefit 'if the entrance (to the town) from the south could be more centrical.'

He demands that

> '... before the site was determined upon, Mr Telford's opinion should be taken, that being (in his opinion) the surest mode of protecting the public, out of whose pockets the whole cost must ultimately come.'

Finally, to the Bridge Committee and Mr Telford in particular, he makes one last appeal: 'Pursue the Line of Conduct so honourably adopted by Mr Brandling (!); treat selfish Scurrility and Abuse with the Contempt it deserves and do your Duty to the Public.'

A third letter (signed 'A Toll-Payer', and dated (Morpeth), November 12th, 1828) was addressed to the Editor of *The Newcastle Chronicle* and was printed in the issue of November 15th.

He brings new light to the problem but regrets that such a degree of dissension should have arisen over the siting of the 'New Bridge', particularly as this might well have jeopardised the very construction of the bridge. For this heated and often acrimonious state of affairs he lays the blame, 'fairly and squarely', at the door of the Bridge Committee.

He gives his reasons: The Committee originally considered three sites and ordered them to be surveyed: the site of the old gaol, that of the present bridge and one, immediately below it, through the House of Correction. It was generally understood and accepted, he says, that one of these was to be the site of the 'New Bridge'.

Then, at the last meeting of the Committee, a fourth proposed site was suddenly introduced. This site, above the Town Hall, was ordered to be surveyed and, apparently, received considerable backing from the limited numbers present at the meeting of the Bridge Committee.

It was this 'last minute' proposal which had given cause to much angry discussion and had destroyed, 'overnight', as it were, the harmony and goodwill existing hitherto.

'Toll-Payer' then makes several points shared by his fellow protester, 'An Inhabitant of Morpeth', regarding the difficulties such a plan would present and the unacceptable expense involved.

Period IV 1830–39

But, unlike the other two correspondents, whose complaints were also published, 'Toll-Payer' proposes a way out of the dilemma that is so dividing the town and causing such 'unnecessary strife.'

Before quarrelling over the site of the 'New Bridge', ought it not to be sensible to establish (perhaps by means of a public enquiry) whether a *new* bridge was actually needed?

He accepts that the present bridge is both 'confessedly dangerous' and 'a disgrace to the county' ('Publicola's description), but asks if it is not capable of improvement, since it might easily be widened and 'by opening out and levelling the approaches to it, it might be made a very good bridge.' He further makes the telling point that such a scheme should be seriously investigated (even at this late stage) since the practicability of his plan would not cost a quarter as much as a new bridge on *any* of the sites proposed. 'Toll-Payer' insists that should a new bridge unfortunately be found to be necessary, then (like the other two correspondents) he believes it to be the duty of the Committee to ensure it costs no more than absolutely necessary. His letter continues in a similar vein, protesting at the expense of making a new line of road and describing the idea of a toll as 'oppressive', insisting that if the expenditure on a new bridge were kept 'to its lowest point', the toll could be 'as light and speedily removed as possible.'

It is important to note that these three letters were written and published before either the article referring to both the meeting of the Bridge Committee and the siting of the bridge, in particular (and composed, one supposes, by a member of the newspaper's reporting staff), appeared in *The Newcastle Courant*, on November 29th; or the letter from Henry Brumell (written on December 2nd), addressed to the Editor of *The Newcastle Courant*, and printed in the edition on December 6th, 1828. The part of the article (of November 29th) dealing with the siting of the bridge says: 'The (new) site runs parallel to the east side of the present bridge and the range of houses at the north end of the bridge (including the Grammar School) is to be pulled down and the whole of the houses on the south side of the river, as far as the old House of Correction.' Brumell's letter (of December 6th) also refers to the meeting of the Bridge Committee, held in the Queen's Head Inn, Morpeth, on 26th of November and states that Thomas Telford's plan, 'which places the new bridge between the House of Correction and the premises on the opposite line of the river ... situated a little to the east of the present bridge', was ordered to be lodged with the Clerk of the Peace.

Both statements, regarding the siting of the bridge are substantially in agreement and both, in fact, are correct, since this is precisely where the bridge *is* situated – though how two people present at the same meeting could not agree on whose plan was adopted by the Committee (Telford's or Dobson's), almost beggars belief! Be that as it may, whether the plan was Telford's or Dobson's, this was the site finally agreed upon.

The 'New Bridge'

Whether the site had already been agreed upon prior to the publication of the three letters from our extremely indignant citizens, we have no means of knowing. Whether the interesting and factually aware correspondences had any influence on the Committee's decision, again, we shall never know.

It is generally accepted that the site for the 'New Bridge', across the River Wansbeck, into Morpeth, was chosen by the road engineer, Thomas Telford. What has always remained less certain is who should receive credit for the bridge's design – Telford or the Newcastle architect, John Dobson?

Much of the (limited) information available regarding the bridge is to be found in the papers of William Woodman, a Morpeth solicitor (born March 9th, 1806), themselves to be found in the *Morpeth Collectanea*, the property of the Society of Antiquaries and now housed in the Northumberland County Records Office in Gosforth.

A letter from Henry Brumell (also a Morpeth solicitor), written on the 2nd December, 1828 (and published in the issue of December 6th), to the Editor of *The Newcastle Courant* (Ref. *Morpeth Collectanea* (1826–39): Vol. 3, p. 15) complains:

> 'The paragraph in your last paper, respecting Morpeth Bridge, is quite incorrect.
> It is certainly true that *Mr Dobson did exhibit a plan* to the committee on the 26th July, *but it was by no means adopted.*
> On the contrary, that which had been sent in by Mr Telford and which places the New Bridge between the House of Correction and the premises on the opposite line of the river … situated a little to the east of the present bridge, was ordered to be lodged with the Clerk of the Peace.'

A letter (according to Brumell), had been sent to Thomas Telford, by the Hon. H. T. Liddell, M.P. (under the direction of the Bridge Committee), enquiring whether a site more suitable for the construction of the bridge than that specified by Telford in his report might possibly be found, but at the time of Brumell's letter (i.e. December 2nd) no reply had yet been received from Mr Telford.

However, 'Mr Telford's plan', the letter concludes, 'has since been lodged in the Clerk of the Peace's Office'.

The article which preceded Henry Brumell's letter (and which, incidently, was published in the issue of December 6th) and which aroused the indignation of the worthy Morpeth solicitor, had appeared in the *Courant* on November the 29th; it reads:

> 'On Wednesday last (November 26th) a numerous meeting of the subscribers and others interested in a new bridge at Morpeth was held at the Queen's Head Inn there, the Hon. H. T. Liddell, M.P. in the chair, to fix upon a site.
> *Two plans by Mr Dobson* and one from Mr Telford *were submitted to the meeting and*, after being minutely examined, *one of Mr Dobson's was agreed upon*, without a division, *as the most eligible.*
> The new site runs parallel to the east side of the present bridge and the range of houses at the north end of the bridge, including the Grammar School, is to be pulled down and the whole of the houses on the south side of the river as far as the old House of Correction.

Period IV 1830–39

The turnpike road, from the church to the new gaol, is likewise to be altered and levelled. The estimated expense of this desirable undertaking is only £8000.'

These two 'articles' clearly refer to the siting of the bridge and not to its design, but when we read the article in the *Courant* (on November 29th) and Henry Brumell's disclaimer, published the following week, far from clarifying the situation, they actually contribute to the argument of who did choose the site for the bridge.

The newspaper report and the solicitor's reply directly and totally contradict each other – one or the other has to be mistaken: either Dobson's plan was adopted or it was not.

What possible motive could the *Courant*'s reporter (who had presumably attended the meeting in Morpeth on November 26th) have for deliberately and convincingly making the assertion he does in a statement (Brumell claims) containing such a monumental error of fact?

On the other hand, Henry Brumell (who likewise, one supposes, attended the meeting at the Queen's Head Inn) is equally certain and positive in his contention that Dobson's plan 'was by no means adopted' and that Telford's had been lodged in the office of the Clerk of the Peace.

On the 9th of December, 1828, Henry Brumell wrote to Sir David Smith, Bart. (of Alnwick), as follows:

> 'I beg leave to inform you that at a meeting this day (December 9th) of the Morpeth Bridge Committee ... Mr Telford's plan was adopted and I have, by their direction, written to him to request he will, as soon as possible, send down plans, elevations and estimations of the intended standing ... '

Here again, Henry Brumell is unequivocal in his assertion that it was Telford's plan, not John Dobson's, which was adopted by the Bridge Committee.

On June 20th, 1829, and writing from London, Telford forwarded a lengthy 'specification', detailing his plans for the bridge's construction (materials, dimensions, and so on).

(Ref. *Morpeth Collectanea* (1826–39): Vol. 3, pp. 21 & 22).

Notices inviting tenders were published in the issues of the *Newcastle Courant* on Saturday June 27th and July 11th, 1829, in the *Newcastle Chronicle* on June 27th, July 4th and July 11th, 1829, and in the issue of the *Tyne Mercury*, on Tuesday, July 7th, 1829.

The notice reads as follows:

Morpeth Bridge.
To Builders, Masons, etc.

> 'The Commissioners appointed by the late Act of Parliament, for the erection of a New Bridge at Morpeth, in the county of Northumberland, are ready to receive proposals for the erection

The 'New Bridge'

of a Stone Bridge, of three arches, at that place, and for making a new weir across the River Wansbeck, near the same; and also for making and completing proper roads or approaches to the bridge, at the north and south ends thereof, by pulling down and clearing away, the houses and other buildings in the intended lines of approach. Plans and specifications of the intended works are lodged with and may be seen at the offices of Mr Brumell, in Morpeth, to whom persons desirous of undertaking the same are requested to send their proposals, sealed up, on or before the 14th of July, 1829; in which proposals, the time within which the work will be completed, must be mentioned.

The contractor will be required to furnish all materials and to find sufficient sureties for the due performance of the works, and the upholding of the bridge for seven years from the finishing thereof; and every person sending in a proposal must specify therein, the names, places of abode, and business of his sureties, with their consent to become bound.

'Every person sending in a proposal is requested to specify, in a separate sheet of paper, sealed up, the sum at which the completion of the works will be undertaken, without mentioning his name therein, then to mark the same with some particular work or figure; to send, at the same time, a letter, also sealed up, and marked on the outside, with a similar word or figure, containing his name and the other particulars above required.'

In 1832, the Reverend John Hodgson published his *A History of Morpeth*. The significance of this date is crucial to the argument of who designed the bridge, since the book was published within one year of the opening of the 'New Bridge'. Hodgson writes:

'Morpeth 'New Bridge' is now building (April, 1831) at a short distance below the old one, between the chapel and the mill; and under the authority of an act for that purpose, which received the royal assent, June 1st, 1829 ... *Mr Telford chose or approved the site on which the bridge is building; and the designs for it*, which were finally adopted, *are by Mr Dobson*, architect, of Newcastle.'

Hodgson continues, briefly, to describe the specifications of the bridge, which were explained fully and in detail in his letter from London, on June the 20th, 1829, by Thomas Telford.

(Ref. *Morpeth Collectanea* (1826–39): Vol. 3, pp. 21 & 22).

William Woodman and the Reverend John Hodgson, were, for a time, regular correspondents. Woodman's letters to his religious colleague (of which there are two dozen or so) are to be found in the *Morpeth M.S.S.* pp. 180–205 (N.C.R.O.) and are dated from November 29th, 1830, to December 28th, (1831?) – (Ref. ZAN M 16 11a ... N.C.R.O.). In his letters Woodman gave The Reverend Hodgson details of Morpeth's history, architecture, plans, etc – yet, not once, in any of these letters, does Woodman refer to the 'New Bridge'.

Considering the importance to the town of this construction and the interest and controversy the siting of the bridge had aroused among sections of the population of Morpeth, this seems an extraordinary omission.

The evidence presented so far (and what is available is very much of a sketchy and fragmented nature, with many pieces of the 'jigsaw' missing and too many frustrating 'blind alleys') as to which of the two men designed the bridge would appear to support the claim of Thomas Telford. That he chose the site for the bridge is generally accepted: whether he actually *designed* it would appear a distinct possibility though there is no definite *proof*.

There is incontrovertible *proof* that the contractors were King and Beldon. But then, in 1832, we have the publication of John Hodgson's *A History of Morpeth*.

It is universally recognised that John Hodgson was a man of great wisdom, integrity and perspicacity, highly intelligent and of an unusual enquiring nature, with a wide and lively interest in all manner of subjects.

It seems unlikely, therefore, that, in writing this history of the town with which he was so closely associated, and at the time he did (1831), his information would be inaccurate, for so much of the other detail is correct in every particular.

He had, after all, no personal axe to grind on behalf of John Dobson, nor any quarrel with Thomas Telford.

It seems inconceivable and entirely out of character that he should make any claim for Dobson's involvement if such a claim was erroneous. Equally, it is remarkable (writing at the very time of the bridge's construction, when public interest was at its peak and information so readily available for public scrutiny) that his statement should be so seemingly at odds with the tone of Woodman's other correspondences, which make no mention of Dobson having designed the bridge nor, for that matter, acknowledge any involvement by the Newcastle architect.

Yet John Hodgson's statement is both clear and unequivocal:

'... *the designs for the bridge*, which were finally adopted, *are by Mr Dobson* ...'

Conclusion:

From information available (bearing in mind that we are dealing with a period of time generally notorious for its in accuracy and for poor, often non-existent, written records), it seems reasonable to conclude that,

a) The engineer, Thomas Telford, chose the site for the bridge (... this is generally accepted with evidence to support the assumption).

b) Thomas King and William Beldon were the contractors who actually built the bridge (... proof for this assertion is to be found on the two stone tablets inlaid in the walls on either side of the bridge).

c) The Newcastle architect, John Dobson, designed the bridge. The evidence supporting this claim is found in the testimony of the Reverend John Hodgson, writing in his *A History of Morpeth*, at the time when the bridge was actually under construction.

It is unimaginable to believe that Hodgson would make this contention if it were not true.

The 'New Bridge'

The New Bridge, Morpeth, Northumberland

'The town proper (Morpeth) clusters round the stumps of a medieval bridge and its handsome, John Dobson successor; built in 1831.'

(Ref. p. 172 of Herbert L. Honeyman's *Northumberland: the County Books Series*).

'A few yards below (the site of the 13th c. bridge, which is now gone and was eventually replaced by a footbridge in 1869, "erected by public subscription" and built by Swinney Brothers of Morpeth) is the "New Bridge", built in 1829-31, with three arches.

The site of the bridge was chosen by Thomas Telford but the design and building were carried out by John Dobson of Newcastle. It replaced a wooden bridge, erected about 1821, to carry materials over the River Wansbeck, for the prison that Dobson was building nearby.'

(Ref. Frank Graham *The Bridges of Northumberland and Durham* 1975; p. 51).

Eldon Square, Newcastle upon Tyne

Eldon Square (Newcastle upon Tyne)

'The houses in Eldon Square were built:

> "to an elevation designed by Mr Dobson ..."

'Eldon Square was Dobson's first known attempt at designs of town terraces, his previous practice having been entirely in the alteration and enlargement of country houses and the design of Presbyterian and Methodist chapels. It is one of his best and we cannot now regret his poaching on what might have been (Thomas) Oliver's preserve.' (Ref. *Archeologia Aeliana* (4th series): Vol. XXIX, p. 250).

The Church of St James, Benwell, Newcastle upon Tyne

The Church of St James (Benwell, Newcastle upon Tyne)

> '(It was) erected as a Chapel of Ease in the Parochial Chapter of St John, in the Parish of St Nicholas. The architect was John Dobson and the church was consecrated in 1832.'

(Ref. *A Guide to the Anglican Churches in Newcastle and Northumberland*).

St Nicholas' Cathedral Church (Newcastle upon Tyne)

Margaret Jane Dobson's catalogue of her father's work in her *Memoir* (1885) is as follows:

> 1819 – Restored the steeple and designed the large, floral Gothic window in the north transept.

> 1832 – Restored the tower's foundations and the north and south porches.

> 'The lantern tower of Newcastle Cathedral (completed in 1448) ... is justly described by Mackenzie (in his *Descriptive and Historical Account of Newcastle upon Tyne*, 1827) as "one of the noblest and most admired structures that adorn our island".'

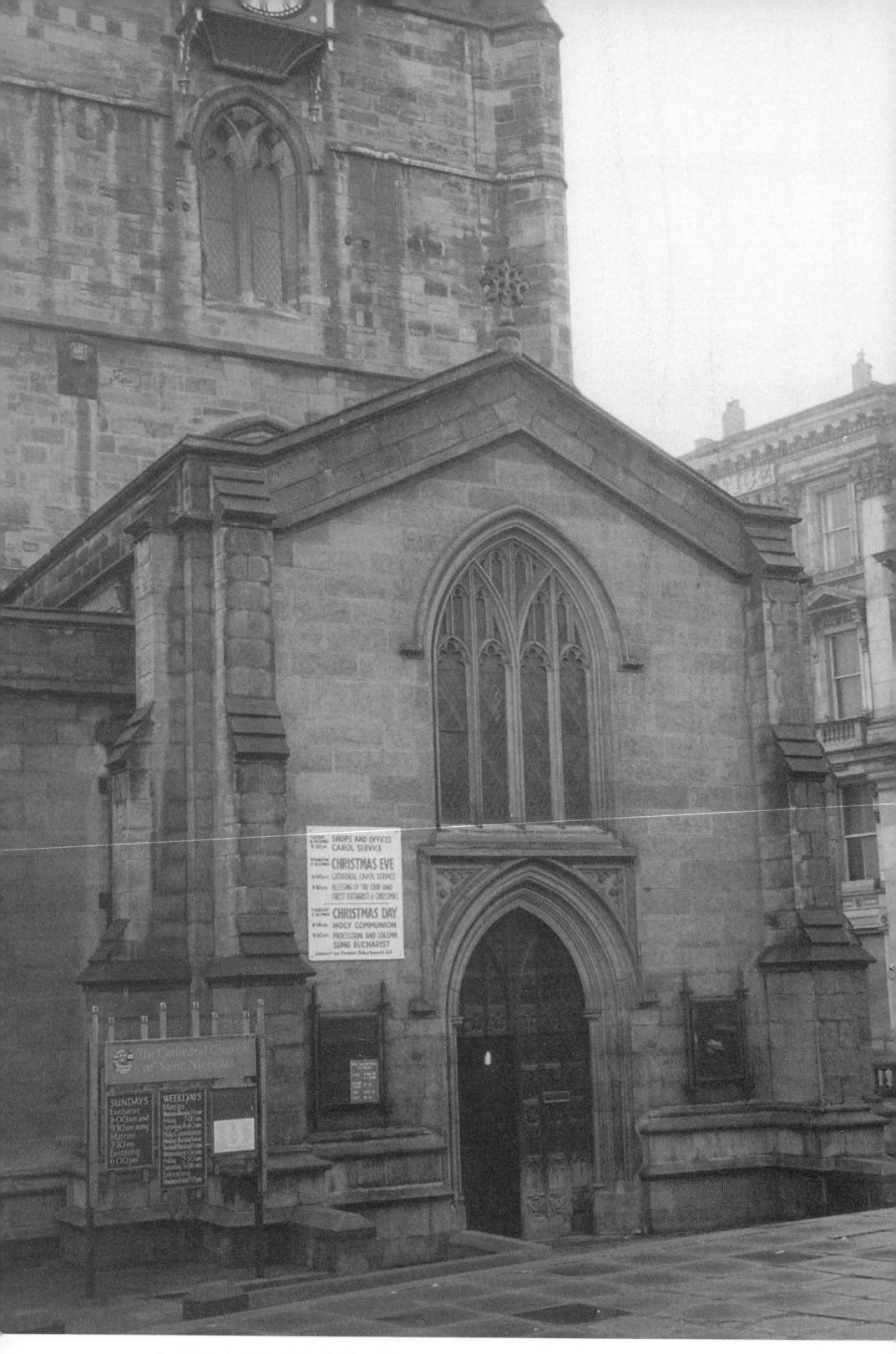

St Nicholas' Cathedral Church, Newcastle upon Tyne, the North-west Porch

St Nicholas' Cathedral Church, Newcastle upon Tyne

(Ref. Allsopp and Clark's *Historic Architecture of Northumberland and Newcastle upon Tyne*, p. 20).

> 'When the lantern tower ... which Robert Stephen calculated weighed seventy tons, was in danger of collapse, Dobson, in circumstances of difficulty and some danger, succeeded in widening the foundations of the 194 feet tower, supporting the walls by buttresses, taking down and restoring the pinnacles and all parts of the superstructure destroyed by age, and was particularly proud of the fact that nothing was to be seen, externally, of this restoration.'

(Ref. *John Dobson, Architect and Landscape Gardener*, pp. 68–9: Lyall Wilkes).

> 'The tower of St Nicholas' Church, which is the pride of Newcastle, was in imminent danger of falling, through the cutting away (by the cupidity of those having a vested interest in the interment fee) of the piers which supported the whole structures.
>
> Mr Dobson took in hand to stay the ruin and actually underset the foundation of a tower 194 feet high, supported the walls by buttresses, which he metamorphosed into a convenient Gothic porch, and took down and restored the pinnacles and other parts of the superstructure decayed by age, and of all this work, executed under circumstances of great difficulty, no trace but the porticos and the buttresses can be detected by an ordinary observer.
>
> In 1827, John Dobson restored the steeple (Sykes, II: p. 213).

(Ref. *The Newcastle Daily Chronicle*: Monday, January 9th 1865).

Blenkinsopp Hall, Haltwhistle, Northumberland

Blenkinsopp Hall (Haltwhistle, Northumberland)

Photographed by kind permission of Mrs L. M. Joicey.

It is said that early in 19th c. the Hall was largely rebuilt, with a long, two-layered (south) front of five bays and that John Dobson 'probably' added a south-east tower ... together with other substantial additions. Despite claims that Dobson's additions have since been demolished, the present owner, Mrs L. M. Joicey, in a letter to me (dated 17th August, 1998) writes 'The part that was pulled down in 1950 was, in fact, only built *c.* 1899 so, if the earlier part was built by John Dobson, most of it survives.'

Blenkinsopp Hall, Haltwhistle, Northumberland

The Grainger Market, Newcastle upon Tyne

The Grainger Market *(Newcastle upon Tyne)*

Newe House, or Anderson Place, as it was re-named by its builder owner, was a mansion started in 1580 in the style of a country seat, right in the middle of a crowded walled town.

By the 1830's, however, despite its apparent grandeur, it had obviously become an anachronism, and if Richard Grainger's ambitious plans for extensive town-centre developments were to be carried through, then it had to go. Grainger presented his plans to the Corporation while, in fact, he was still negotiating the purchase of Anderson Place with the late George Anderson's son, Thomas.

He eventually secured its purchase for the sum of £50,000. This site was to be the heart of his commercial and residential development: a network of streets and a covered market designed by John Dobson.

In 1834 the Corporation (encouraged by John Clayton, the Town Clerk) did indeed accept Grainger's plans and on the 24th of October, 1835, at a cost of £36,290, within one year of the contract being signed, the Markets were officially opened.

They were the most successful attempt at a traffic-free shopping precinct Newcastle has ever achieved, not only because owing to the low rents and overheads they could (and still can) sell goods cheaper than shops in the main streets.

> 'The whole was contained within four streets of shops and houses "surpassing anything in street architecture hitherto witnessed in this neighbourhood"'

(*Newcastle Journal*: 31st october, 1835).

Many traders moved here from the Quayside, keen to take advantage of the new developments – at the same time accelerating the decline of the riverside.

Dobson's enormous covered market, protected by a massive glass roof, was the largest in the country and of great architectural elegance. It covers several acres and the interior consists of five longitudinal avenues and four transverse ones, each twelve feet wide, and they 'present a succession of arched passages between the larger avenues.'

Newcastle General Cemetery (*Jesmond Road, Newcastle upon Tyne*)

'The laying out of the new cemetery at Jesmond, Newcastle, afforded Mr Dobson scope for

Newcastle General Cemetery, Jesmond Road, Newcastle upon Tyne

Above: *Newcastle General Cemetery, the cemetery gates.*

Right: *Newcastle General Cemetery, the south entrance*

Period IV 1830-39

the display of his ability both as an architect and a landscape gardener and the result is well worthy the attention of the student as an excellent example.'

(Ref. *The Builder*; January 14th, 1865).

'In 1834, the handsome chapels and entrance gate of the Jesmond Cemetery were the result of his skill.'

(Ref. *The Newcastle Daily Journal*; January 9th, 1865).

John Dobson designed the Cemetery Gates and was responsible for the laying out of the entire cemetery.

His daughter, writing in her *Memoir*, of 1885, expressed the view that 'the cemetery is ornamentally laid out and yet there is no mistaking it for a mere garden'.

Opposite Bottom: The south entrance: and the two massive gate piers.

Low Ford Bridge *(Morpeth, Northumberland)*

A notice appeared in *The Newcastle Chronicle* of Saturday, May 2nd, 1835 and in *The Newcastle Courant* of that same date, addressed to 'Builders': it read:

'The erection of a Bridge, across the River Wansbeck, at the Low Ford, near to Morpeth, being under the Direction and Management of a Committee formed in that Town and Neighbourhood: Proposals will be received by them, at the Queen's Head Inn, Morpeth, between the hours of ten and twelve, on Wednesday, the 13th day of May, next.

Low Ford Bridge, Morpeth, Northumberland

Grey Street (East Side), Newcastle upon Tyne

Plans and Specification may be seen by applying to Mr Wilkinson, Stationer, Morpeth; or Mr Dobson, Architect, Newcastle.

The notice in the *Chronicle* is dated April 22nd, 1835: that in the *Courant* is dated one week later, on the 29th of April.

The bridge crosses the River Wansbeck on the road between Morpeth and Mitford. Pevsner and Richmond (*The Buildings of England: Northumberland*, p. 398) described it as 'plain and simple': 1836, by John Dobson.

Grey Street (East Side) *(Newcastle upon Tyne)*

The honey-coloured building in the centre of the picture was once Martin's Bank (18–26 Grey Street). Built around 1836 by John Dobson for Richard Grainger, the ground floor is the work of W. L. Newcombe (*c.* 1890).

Brinkburn Priory Church of St Peter *(Northumberland)* and St Paul

Brinkburn was already known by that name when, in the reign of Henry I, William de Bertram of Mitford selected it for the site of a Convent of Austen Canons (about the year 1135).

Brinkburn Priory Church and above, the Priory House

Brinkburn Priory Church of St Peter and St Paul, the north side

With the consent of his wife and sons, he commissioned Osbert Coluntarius to begin building for Sir Ralph the priest and his brethren.

The Bertrams made valuable grants of land to the Priory but the 'Chartulary' (a register or record book kept in a monastery) shows they were often impoverished by Scottish raids.

Legend has it that on one occasion the Scots had been unable to find the Priory, hidden among the thick woodland, and so the marauders turned their horses northwards. The monks, grateful for their deliverance, rang the deep bells of the monastery in their relief.

Alas, the sound of the bell guided the raiders back to leave behind them fire and slaughter in the peaceful valley. The canons complained often and long (and with good reason) about their poverty – a Commissioners' report of 1552 supported their complaint.

In 1556, however, the Prior was found guilty of immoral conduct and his canons guilty of 'venerating a girdle of St Peter'.

The convent was dissolved and the Prior, William Hodgson, was dismissed with an annual pension of eleven pounds.

After the Dissolution, the Priory passed into lay hands and a house was established on the site. The church remained in use but began to decay (in the 17th c. the roof of the Priory fell in at the south-west angle) and regular services lapsed in 1683, although burials continued.

Despite its troubles, Brinkburn remained a beautiful blending of the richest Norman work with purest Early English.

It is earlier than Hexham Abbey and it is possible its lancet windows have been copied in many churches in South Northumberland.

(Ref. p. 308 of P. Anderson Graham's *Highways and Byways in Northumbria*).

On page 102 of Faulkner & Greg's *John Dobson, Newcastle Architect, 1787–1865*, we read that (John Dobson) carried out 'repairs to the ruined Priory for Major William Hodgson-Cadogan, *c.* 1830–7: fully restored by Thomas Austin, 1858'.

(*HMBCE* guide, 1985).

W. W. Tomlinson, in his *Comprehensive Guide to Northumberland*, tells a fascinating short story:

> 'During some excavations to the south-west corner of the church, in 1834–5, a copper jug of Edwardian character was unearthed, containing nearly three hundred gold coins, of the reigns of Edward III, Richard II and Henry IV.'

John Dobson's work at Brinkburn began in 1830 and ended in 1837.

Tomlinson described it as 'a large cruciform edifice, 131 feet in length, having a nave of six bays with a north aisle; transepts with aisles on the east; a chancel and a low, square, central tower, upborne on lofty and well-proportioned arches.'

Photographed by kind permission of English Heritage.

Brinkburn Priory House (*Northumberland*)

The Newcastle Daily Journal of January 16th, 1865 reports that John Dobson made large additions to the house (of *c.* 1800), for Major William Hodgson-Cadogan: (drawings can be seen in the Laing Art Gallery, Newcastle).

Brinkburn Priory House, Northumberland, Gateway looking west

Above: *Brinkburn Priory House, Northumberland. Dobson inserted the huge bow, with its six Georgian-Gothic windows, into the original east side of the house. The large central windows, with their intersecting tracery, match those on either side of the bow in everything but size.*

Left: *Brinkburn Priory House, south side of the house (facing the River Coquet). Photographed with kind permission of English Heritage.*

Grey Street, 'The Curve', Newcastle upon Tyne

Grey Street (Newcastle upon Tyne)

The Newcastle Journal of June 8th. 1837, referred to the most beautiful and elaborately designed side of Grey Street (the west side) ... in terms which succeeding generations of architectural historians have chosen to ignore: '... it is but justice to say [they] have been entirely designed (i.e. the buildings on the west side) in Mr Grainger's office, by Mr Wardle, under Mr Grainger's immediate directions.'

(*Tyneside Portraits*, Lyall Wilkes: p. 117).

This claim on Wardle's behalf is borne out by a letter in the *Newcastle Daily Chronicle* (March 21st, 1868), signed 'Veritas', which reads:

> 'The Butcher and Green Markets ... were designed by the late Mr Dobson, who also designed that portion of the east side of Grey Street which reaches from Shakespeare Street to Mosely Street – all the rest of the new streets, including part of Grey Street (presumably the west side referred to much earlier in the *Newcastle Journal* of 8th June, 1837), Grainger Street, Market Street, Clayton Street, etc, etc, were designed by the late Mr John Wardle.'

If this information and its correspondent is correct, than this most certainly refutes the claims made by Dobson's daughter, Miss Margaret Jane Dobson, on page 67 of her *Memoir*, in which she claims ...

> 'Mr Dobson furnished designs for a great portion of Grey Street, serving as a model to Mr Grainger's clerks for the rest.'

To her father she later ascribes credit for the designs of Market Street, Hood Street, Nun Street, Grainger Street, Grey Street, etc.

In any event and to whoever be credited the glory, few would argue with W. E. Gladstone (1809–98) writing in his diary on 7th October, 1862:

> '... Grey Street – I think our best modern street.'

Holy Trinity Church, now Trinity Community Centre, Gateshead

Holy Trinity Church *(now Trinity Community Centre, Gateshead)*

St Edmunds's Chapel was restored for worship, in 1837, by John Dobson. It has a fascinating 13th c. front.

The impressive doorway has two tiers of (two) 'blanked' arches. Above these and right across the face of the building is a group of seven beautiful, lancet 'stepped' arches – three with windows and four without.

Chesters *(Humshaugh, Hexham, Northumberland)*

'(John Dobson made) additions to John Carr's house (of 1771), for John Clayton, 1832–37: remodelled by R. Norman Shaw, 1893:'

(Ref. p. 87 of Margaret Jane Dobson's *Memoir* (1885)). Photographed by kind permission of Mr George Benson.

Chesters, Humshaugh, Hexham, Northumberland

Chesters, Humshaugh, Hexham, Northumberland

Holme Eden Abbey, Warwick Bridge, Cumbria

Holme Eden Abbey   *(Warwick Bridge, Cumbria)*

In its appearance it reminds one very much of Beaufront Castle, Hexham. Built, by John Dobson in 1837, using the local, red sandstone, it is raised on a terrace overlooking the River Eden.

Holme Eden Abbey was built between 1833–37 and was designed by John Dobson. It is a spectacular essay in red sandstone, notable for its Tudor elevations, towers, turrets and crenellations as well as an interior that celebrates the plasterer's and the gilder's art.

Conceived as a 'calendar house' (it has 365 windows, 52 chimneys, 12 corridors, 4 floors and seven exits), it is only one of two such houses in the entire country. Holme Eden is a Grade II listed building.

Constructed in the Tudor style, this sumptuous mansion bristles with ornamental chimneys, high mullioned windows, a crenellated porch stairway landing and cantilevered balcony. Many of the reception rooms have vaulted or coffered ceilings, some finely decorated and gilded, and there are dressed stone fireplaces with beautiful ceramic tile inserts.

All interior stone and woodwork is of the finest quality.

1. 'mullion': a vertical member between the lights (i.e. the compartments of a window) in a window opening.
2. 'cantilever': a large bracket used in architecture for supporting cornices, balconies and even stairs – the principle has been applied in the construction of bridges to support enormous weights.
3. 'coffers' sunken panels (square or polygonal) decorating a ceiling, vault or arch.

The house was built for Peter Dixon Junior, who was one of three sons (John, George and Peter Junior) of Peter Dixon the elder, who himself was the son of a wealthy customs officer and was born in Whitehaven in 1753. In 1809 the family firm of Peter Dixon & Sons took over a newly built cotton factory, Lanthwaite Mill, at Warwick Bridge, and their business flourished. The effects of the

Holme Eden Abbey, showing the main entrance

Industrial Revolution ensured that the individual members of the family all became wealthy men.

Peter Senior bought a town-house in Carlisle, Tullie House, which today is an award-winning museum and art gallery.

Peter Junior (the most flamboyant member of the family) built what was then described as a virtual palace ... Holme Eden.

It opened its doors for an inaugural ball in 1837.

Yet despite their wealth and the success of their business enterprises, their good fortune lasted barely thirty years.

Peter Dixon Senior died in 1832, John in 1857 and George three years later; but it was the after-effects of the American Civil War (1860–65) which were eventually to destroy both the business and the health of Peter Dixon. He died in 1866 and the business collapsed in 1872.

In 1873, following the demise of Peter Dixon's fortunes, the estate was auctioned in several lots, the mansion and 51 surrounding acres being bought by a Cumbrian family trust. However, after a time the trust ceased to function and Holme Eden was again placed on the market, this time with a recommendation that it be torn down and its fabric sold off as building material.

Learning of its imminent fate, a local landowner stepped in and bought the mansion, even though he had no use for it.

Holme Eden remained within his benevolent protection for the next eight years, during which time the strongest expression of interest in the property came from a Carlisle company intent on turning the mansion into a sausage factory!

Having saved it from one fate only to be faced with another of arguably greater humiliation, the landowner took the decision to consign Home Eden into the hands of God and he bequeathed it to the Benedictine Order. For the next sixty years Holme Eden was a convent, home to sixty nuns, who undertook crafts and manual work, illumination, church work, weaving, modelling and any other kind of work for the common good – indoor or outdoor. It numbered Cardinal Basil Hume amongst its famous visitors. Now known as Holme Eden Abbey, the mansion provided what the Order described as 'the ideal, tranquil haven, in which to enjoy the inward peace which Our Lord promised to His disciples, in the fulfilment of the Benedictine ideal – the reintegration of the whole person in Christ.'

In 1983 the Mother Superior died. With only eight nuns still resident, the Order decided to sell and the property was acquired by the present owner, Mrs Doreen Parsons.

A major renovation programme was instituted immediately. All the original keynote features of Dobson's grand design were lovingly preserved, most notably the magnificent stone central staircase; panelled doors with moulded architraves; window shutters; Minster stone fireplaces; plaster panelled ceilings with frieze carving and gilded reliefs. Also retained was the extensive cellarage and – a typical Dobson flourish – a tunnel housing six-stall stabling, leading from the rear of the house to its courtyard and the Coach House, Bake House and storage buildings. Holme Eden functioned as a highly successful residential retirement home until December 1996, when Mrs Parsons herself decided to retire.

Photographed by kind permission of Mrs D. H. Parsons.

John Dobson – and the streets of 'Grainger Town'.

'On October 5th, 1835, the Common Council named the new streets – Clayton (after the Town Clerk); Grainger (for fairly obvious reasons); Market (because it ran from Pilgrim Street to the entrance to the 'Grainger Market'); Shakespeare (because it was to include the Theatre Royal in its length ...); Hood (after a late Mayor); Nun (because of its siting); Nelson (?); and Upper Dean Street (because that, in fact, was what it was until Earl Grey was honoured at a special meeting of the Town Council, on 14th February, 1836).'

(Ref. Wilkes and Dodds' *Tyneside Classical*, pp. 77–78).

Trying, however, to discover which architect was responsible for which street in 'Grainger Town' is an almost impossible task.

Time and again, when reading the commentaries and opinions of those qualified to give sound informed judgement, the same uncertainties repeatedly present themselves: 'evidence suggests that', 'perhaps', 'it is more than likely', 'this might be true', and the reservation recurring more than any other: 'probably'.

Let us examine what these different 'authorities' have said on the vexed question of which architect planned and/or designed these different streets, while at the same time tying to appreciate the difficulties they faced in attempting to form their judgements.

Period IV 1830–39

Margaret Jane Dobson's claim on her father's behalf (in her *Memoir* of 1885) is clear and unequivocal:

'Planned, Levelled and Designed Elevations for

Grey Street	1834–37
Market Street	1835
Hood Street	1836
Grainger Street	1836
Nelson Street	1835
Planned Neville Street	(no date is offered).

The Tyneside Classical Tradition, p. 20, has this to say on the subject:

'The identity of the architects for the various parts of Grainger's scheme is, in many instances, still in debate.

The remarkable unity of each street and the careful hierarchy of decoration, from Grey Street down to the stark simplicity of West Clayton Street, suggests an overall vision that was *probably* Grainger's own; but the names of Newcastle's architects have been attached to several portions.

We know that John Dobson was responsible for the New Markets and John and Benjamin Green for the Theatre Royal and *probably* the other façades of that block (their drawings are in the Metropolitan Museum of Art in New York).

Contemporary sources refer to the two previously unmentioned figures, George Walker and John Wardle, and it is more than likely that Thomas Oliver, following his successful collaboration with Grainger on the Leazes Terrace scheme, would also have been involved.

Serious attributions based on style have not yet been made but what little contemporary evidence there is *suggests* that Wardle was responsible for the West side of Grey Street and the continuation of this façade into Market Street and Grainger Street and the South side of Shakespeare Street. Dobson designed the East side of Grey Street, below the Theatre Royal.'

Lyall Wilkes and Gordon Dodds, in their book, *Tyneside Classical*, p. 95, offer this opinion:

'... whilst research (into material of the 1830s) has certainly not shown that Dobson did *not* design Grey Street and Grainger Street, there exists evidence which suggests that others certainly had a hand in the designs. There is no reliable evidence suggesting that Dobson was the sole designer. Original plans and designs appear to have been destroyed: the further one gets in time from the date of building, the more boldly it is asserted that Dobson was the sole designer; the nearer one gets to the years of actual building, the more suggestions appear that other hands and minds were involved as well.'

On p. 487 of the 1992 (revised) edition of Pevsner and Richmond's *The Buildings of England: Northumberland*, we read that:

'Despite the impression given in *A Memoir of John Dobson* (1885) by his daughter Margaret, Dobson was *not* the principle architect (of Grey Street). 19th c. evidence *suggests* that he designed the East side between Mosley and Shakespeare Streets and that John and Benjamin Green designed the whole block between Market and Shakespeare Streets (which includes the Theatre Royal). John Wardle and George Walker, who began their partnership in Grainger's office, designed the remainder and also all the other streets in the scheme, with the exception of the interior and *perhaps* the exterior of Grainger Market – which was by Dobson.

John Dobson – and the streets of 'Grainger Town'.

David Bean (*Newcastle 900*, p. 44) 'muddies the waters' even further:

'On Christmas Day, 1834 ... Neville Street ... was inaugurated ... and the Subscription Band led a procession along it, in which John Dobson was drawn along it in a chariot.

Grainger Street, Market Street and their tributaries Hood, Shakespeare, Nelson and Nun – all followed in the next few years.

'It seemed that Grainger and Dobson had taken over Newcastle.'

Lyall Wilkes, in his *Tyneside Portraits*, p. 126, quotes the Editor of *The Newcastle Journal* (3rd June, 1837) who wrote:

'... the western half of Market Street and Grainger Street, it is but justice to say, have been entirely designed in Mr Grainger's office by Mr Wardle – under Mr Grainger's immediate directions.'

In the same article the Editor goes on to say that Wardle designed the South side of Shakespeare Street and that the North side was designed by John and Benjamin Green.'

Wilkes then makes a telling and very important observation: 'There was no dissent from these statements in the succeeding issues of *The Newcastle Journal* when there was greater interest in who deserved the credit for the beauty of the new streets than at any subsequent time and when all the claimants for the honour were alive and working in the town.'

Thus far, then, there is some general agreement on specific parts of 'the Town' and conjecture on others.

The comments of the Editor of *The Newcastle Journal*, written so very near the period of construction, are extremely valid and must be considered seriously; for it seems likely that had his statement been factually open to question, then surely objections would have been raised within a few days of its publication. Wilkes assures us that no such objections were raised.

There remains doubt in my mind as to which architect designed Hood Street, Nun Street and Nelson Street, but it seems doubtful we shall ever be sure. The street façades of the Grainger Market 'block' (accounting for Nelson and Nun Streets) have been credited to Dobson but can we be absolutely sure?

Tyneside Classical tells us '... original plans and designs appear to have been destroyed', and clearly herein lies the root of the problem.

Another contributing factor (rather paradoxically) to the scene of confusion may possibly be that throughout the 19th c. Newcastle happened to be blessed with so many fine, talented architects of outstanding ability – Thomas Oliver, John and Benjamin Green, John Wardle, George Walker and, of course, John Dobson, whose architectural styles were not so very dissimilar.

Indeed, there had never been in the town's history so many able designer-architects, all well versed in classical architecture, thanks largely to the tradition and example of men like David Stephenson[1], John and William Stokoe[2], Sir Charles Monck[3] and James Paine[4].

As a rather simplistic theory this may be wide of the mark but it may account for the fact that other architects' work is sometimes mistaken for Dobson's. Thomas Oliver was Dobson's assistant from 1813–21 and must surely have learned much of Dobson's style (it is not unusual in music, in painting and in literature for the pupil's work to be eventually confused with that of the 'master'; why should it be any different with students of architecture?).

John Wardle's Hancock Museum (Barras Bridge), of 1878, has been described as 'almost unbelievably Dobsonian for that date, with Dobson's beautiful ashlar, his Doric pilasters and heavy attic and even the sans-serif capital letters of the pre-Victorian 19th c.'

Margaret Jane Dobson adamantly claims her father designed the streets mentioned earlier.

She concedes that 'Mr Wardle and Mr Walker ... were both men of talent,' but in the same breath accuses them of 'judiciously incorporating Mr Dobson's designs into their own work.'

The argument and speculation continues. For the sake of historical accuracy, it seems a pity there is no definitive record or explanation of who actually designed the streets of 'Grainger Town', but there is not.

Moreover, if 'experts' still cannot agree, then it is surely an impossible task for an amateur to disentangle these intriguing conundrums, an ongoing tale of mystery and perplexity.

Perhaps Lyall Wilkes (in his *John Dobson, Architect and Landscape Gardener*, p. 22) deserves the final verdict:

> 'Dobson is too good an architect, with too many beautiful buildings to his credit ... to need the attribution to him of works he did not do.'

1. David Stephenson (1757–1819): 'architect of All Saints Church, Newcastle and for a time considered the town's senior (and, indeed, only!) architect', of whom Dobson said, in his Presidential Address to the Northern Architectural Association (April 19th, 1859): 'I will not say that he was an accomplished architect', but he was a man of excellent character and much kindness of disposition.'

2. John Stokoe (c. 1756–1836), 'and his father, William: designed Elswick Hall and the Moot Hall (Newcastle) and Hartford Hall, near Bedlington, Northumberland.

3. Sir Charles Monck (1779–1867): Dobson expressed real admiration for Monck's work. He introduced a style of masonry previously unknown: he was a man of refined taste.'

    'I consider', said Dobson, 'that the North of England is much indebted to the worthy baronet's enterprise and cultivated taste.'

    Belsay Hall and Linden Hall (Longhorsley) are memorials to Monck's vision, originality and craftsmanship.

4. For James Paine (1717–89) (and between 1745–70 considered the country's leading house-architect), John Dobson (unusually for a man of genial temper, modest and unassuming) has little but scornful contempt. His criticism of Paine in his Presidential Address betrays something of the depth of bitterness and even anger that he felt for the man: (see notes accompanying photographs of Belford Hall).

Suffice it here to say he accused Paine of 'effecting no improvement on his predecessor (Sir John Vanbrough) in the interior temperature of houses.' Of Vanbrough he complained that '... his interiors were grand ... but they were accomplished at the sacrifice of convenience and comfort.' And of Seaton Delaval Hall in particular, he reported that in cold weather the building was almost uninhabitable.'

Among Paine's many works are Belford Hall, Axwell Park, Bywell Hall and Gosforth House, as well as important contributions to Gibside, Wallington Hall and Blagdon Hall.

Nun Street *(Newcastle upon Tyne)*

Nun Street, Newcastle upon Tyne, the south side

Nelson Street, Newcastle upon Tyne
Right to left: *The Music Hall of 1838; next to it a warehouse of c. 1899 (built on the site of a Methodist Chapel of 1837); then the Dispensary (later the Fruit Market or Exchange) of 1839; and finally the Cordwainers' Company Meeting Hall (the Cordwainers were one of the important medieval Guilds in Newcastle), again of 1838.*

Nelson Street   *(Newcastle upon Tyne)*

The buildings that make up the east side of Nelson Street are unusual in that they have been individually designed.

The Cordwainers' Hall of 1838. The stone tablet above the central, first-floor windows reads – Cordwainers' Hall. Wardens, Thomas Gilroy and John Walker, MDCCCXXXVIII.

Clayton Street, Newcastle upon Tyne, looking west

Clayton Street (Newcastle upon Tyne)

Craster Tower (Northumberland)

The battlemented, medieval tower (on the left) has two rows of (three) windows, the central, larger window with intersecting tracery. In 1769 the two-and-a-half

Craster Tower, Northumberland

179

Craster Tower, Northumberland
Here we see the beautiful south-front with its open pediment, and the plainer east side with its bay-window, added by Dobson in 1839. Photographed by kind permission of Mrs J. M. Craster and Miss M. D. Cra'ster.

Craster Tower, Northumberland

storeyed, five-bay manor house was built on to the south side of the tower.

The Newcastle Daily Journal of January 16th, 1865, refers to 'minor' alterations to the house made by John Dobson, in 1839.

It has a 'tripartite doorway' with Tuscan pilasters and an open pediment. The Georgian house (faced with local whinstone, though the doorway, window frames and quoins are all of sandstone) is attached to the medieval tower.

In 1837 Thomas Wood-Craster inherited the property and adopted the name. It was probably he who enlarged the garden and created the ha-ha ditch.

PERIOD V
1840–50

(29–48) Carlton Terrace *(Jesmond, Newcastle upon Tyne)*

This rather fine residential terrace has been attributed to John Dobson. First proposed by him in 1820, it was finally built in 1838. The wings and centre project slightly.

(29–48) Carlton Terrace, Jesmond, Newcastle upon Tyne

Boldon House (66–70 Front Street), East Boldon, County Durham

Boldon House (66–70 Front Street) *(East Boldon, County Durham)*

A two-storeyed, five-bay, brick house with hipped roof. The attractive, pedimented doorway has Tuscan columns.

John Dobson, we are told, made minor alterations to the house for William Grey, in 1840. Photographed by kind permission of Mr Donald Graham.

Beaufront Castle *(Hexham, Northumberland)*

Tomlinson tells us that Beaufront Castle '... an elegant building of the domestic castellated style, was built by W. Cuthbert Esq, on the site of a more ancient mansion, which was the seat of the Carnabys in the reign of Queen Elizabeth I ...'

The old hall was surmounted by a battlemented parapet, on which were several figures in stone representing the various heathen deities. Many of these have been preserved and may be seen on the north wall of the present castle.

The tall tower, with the arched doorway and large tripartite window, the main entrance on the west side.

T. H. Rowland writes that W. Cuthbert commissioned John Dobson to build a new house and the architect obliged 'in the grand style'. Dobson was proud of [Beaufront] and 'considered it to be his best work'.

Interestingly, Wilkes tells us that 'At Beaufront there is still William Cuthbert's

Beaufront Castle, Hexham, Northumberland

Beaufront Castle, Hexham, Northumberland

Trinity House, Broad Chare, Newcastle upon Tyne

account book, showing the names of the workmen concerned in the building of the house, the work they did and the amounts they received. The only two amounts shown for Dobson's fees, as architect, total a modest £250 – far less than some craftsmen received!

Frank Graham expresses the view that 'today, Beaufront would not be considered one of Dobson's best buildings.' Photographed by kind permission of Mr J. Aidan Cuthbert.

Trinity House   *(Broad Chare, Newcastle upon Tyne)*

The seventeenth-century houses (the property of Trinity House) on the south side of the Chapel on Broad Chare, had been frequently repaired and altered, so much so that, by the early nineteenth century, it was decided to rebuild two of them.

On the 3rd of May, 1841 John Dobson (the *advising* architect) attended a meeting of 'the Board' (of Trinity House), where he gave his estimate (the sum of £257-15-03) for the dismantling of the remains of the two warehouses and rebuilding them completely, a proposal which was agreed to by the Board.

The work was carried out during 1841. The builder was Richard Cail and his joiner was one Mr McAllister.

John Dobson duly presented the tradesmen's bills for payment as each stage of the work was completed.

The final bill was paid on December the 6th, 1841 to a Mr Oliver (Architect),

Trinity House, In the main courtyard are the Almshouses of 1787.

though whether this was Andrew or Thomas Oliver isn't known '... for drawing plans of the warehouses in Broad Chare.'

Although for many years John Dobson was entered in Trinity House's books as their architect, his continuation appears to have been largely consultative.

The system seems to have been that his office prepared drawings for *minor* alterations only – his role in the rebuilding of the two warehouses, for example, was that of adviser and intermediary, notwithstanding the advertisements (in the *Newcastle Daily Chronicle* of Saturday, April 3rd, 1841), inviting builders to tender for the work, which said: 'Plans of the Buildings and specifications of the various works to be seen at Mr Dobson's office, in Newcastle.'

John Dobson renewed the old doorway and the three cellar windows on the north side of the passage from Broad Chare ...

Trinity House Courtyard, an inner view

Market Keeper's House

Market Keeper's House

In 1492 Ralph Hebborn (a local merchant), after whom Hebburn got its name, donated part of his estate in Broad Chare as a meeting place or 'Trinity House'. The rental for this act of generosity was to be an annual payment (if asked for) of one red rose.

> John Dobson improved the inner archway by covering the old joists above it in the form of an arch.

(Ref. *Archaelogia Aeliana* (Fifth edition): Volume XIII, p. 180.

> 'To step into Trinity House courtyard is like straying into a different, calmer age.'

(Ref. *Newcastle 900*, p. 30: David Bean)
Photographed by kind permission of the Brethren of Trinity House.

Market Keeper's House   (Neville Street, Newcastle upon Tyne)

Print [The Market Keeper's House, Cattle Market, Collard and Ross 1841] of 1841; reproduced by kind permission of Tyne and Wear Development Corporation.

Market Keeper's Cottage, Neville Street, Newcastle upon Tyne

Period V 1840–50

Market Keeper's Cottage, Neville Street, Newcastle upon Tyne

Market Keeper's Cottage (*Neville Street, Newcastle upon Tyne*)

The Market Keeper's Cottage at the top of Scotswood Road, in 1906. Tyne and Wear Development Corporation is restoring the cottage and it will become a focal point within Newcastle's £54 million Millennium project, 'The International Centre for Life'.

This (1906) photograph is reproduced by kind permission of Tyne and Wear Development Corporation.

Referred to by the *Newcastle Daily Journal* (January 16th, 1865) as the 'Market House, Neville Street, Newcastle upon Tyne classical cattle market office and toll house'. It (wrongly) quotes the date as 1831.

I am assured by Mrs Christine Holland, Public Affairs Consultant at the International Centre of Life (of which the Market Keeper's 'House' is a feature), that the correct date is certainly 1841.

Photographed by kind permission of The Tyne and Wear Development Corporation.

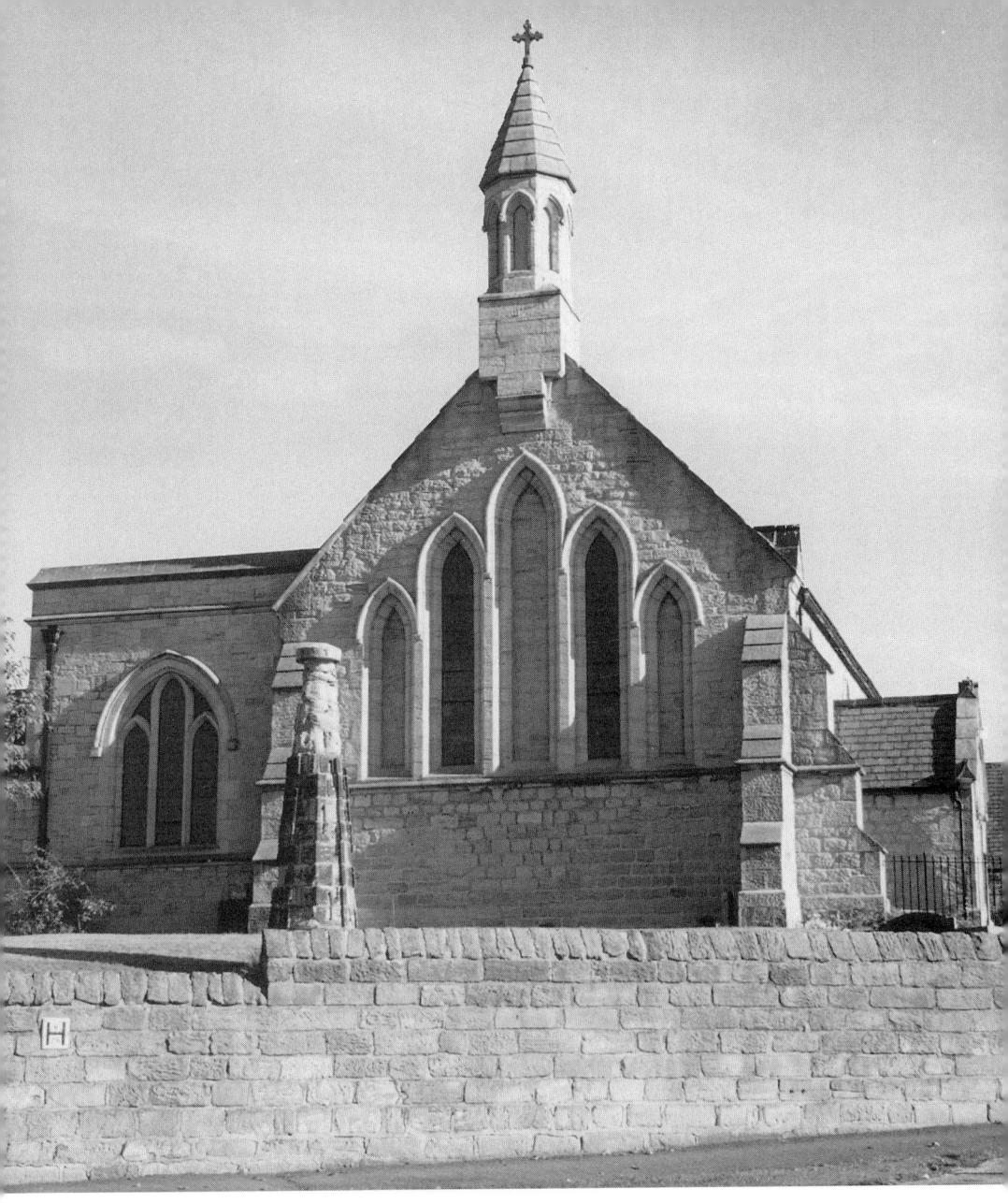

St Joseph's R.C. Church, Birtley, County Durham

St Joseph's R.C. Church (Birtley, County Durham)

The west face of the church is heavily buttressed. It also has five stepped lancet windows – three of them 'blind'. The church is topped by a corbelled bellcote. St Joseph's was designed by John Dobson and built between 1842–44.

The Archibald Reed Monument, Jesmond Cemetery, Newcastle upon Tyne

The Archibald Reed Monument (*Jesmond Cemetery, Newcastle upon Tyne*)

'Gothic tower tomb, c. 1843. memorial to Archibald Reed: Sheriff, Alderman and six times Mayor of Newcastle; died 1842.

Sandstone ashlar, two-stage tower with pinnacled diagonal buttresses and octagonal spire.'

(Ref. *List of Buildings of Special Architectural or Historic Interest*: Department of the Environment, 1987: District of Newcastle, Tyne and Wear).

Hackwood House – formerly 'the Hags', Hexham, Northumberland)

Hackwood House – formerly 'the Hags' *(Hexham, Northumberland)*

The house, like so many others now, is divided into three parts – the main part of the building (which, since 1987 has been owned by Robert and Veronica Wassell), the south wing and the mews.

Photographed by kind permission of Mr and Mrs R. W. Wassell.

The R.C. Church of St Elizabeth, Minsteracres Monastery, Kiln Pit Hill, near Consett, Co. Durham

Minsteracres Monastery *(Kiln Pit Hill, near Consett, Co. Durham)*

The Roman Catholic Church of St Elizabeth (in the Decorated style) was built as a private chapel for the Silvertop family.

There is ample evidence to suggest it was designed by John Dobson, in 1843. Photographed by kind permission of Father Aelred Smith.

St Andrew's Church, Newgate Street, Newcastle upon Tyne

St Andrew's Church (Newgate Street, Newcastle upon Tyne)

'The church was first without transepts and both were added during the 13th c., when larger archways would have been made on each side at the east end of the nave, possibly that on the south side being made before that on the north. The present archway on the south side is that which was erected in 1844, when the south transept was rebuilt.
The original archway would be pointed and similar to that in the north transept.'

(Information source: The notes on St Andrew's, printed in booklet form by Norman Ward Ltd., Kells Lane, Low Fell, Gateshead, Tyne and Wear).

In her *Memoir* of 1885, M.J. Dobson claims her father restored the south transept in 1844, the north transept in 1845, the chancel in 1846, and installed heating in the church in 1848.

Grey, in *Chorographie* or *Survey of Newcastle* (1649) says;

'Saint Andrew's is ancientiest of all the four (city churches), as appeareth by the old building and fashion of the Church.'

As others have also said, the style of the building shows that it is the oldest and so tradition has always held it to be.

(Ref. *Church Notes*: printed by N. Ward Ltd., Kells Lane, Low Fell, Gateshead.)

Haughton Castle, Humshaugh, near Hexham, Northumberland

Haughton Castle

(Humshaugh, near Hexham, Northumberland)

'There must have been a timber hall before the stone castle', suggests T. H. Rowland.

The house, constructed in the reign of Henry III (in the 13th century), was 'a country gentleman's dwelling, not a castle.' It may well have been a single-storeyed house and then had another level added.

The conversion of the old 'hall-house' into a castle was accomplished by Gerald Widdrington, who some time after the death of Adam Swinburne, the

Haughton Castle, Humshaugh, near Hexham, Northumberland

Haughton Castle, entrance on the east front

previous owner (who died *c.* 1317), married one of Swinburne's daughters and thus came into possession of the 'hall'.

He built up the (five) arched recesses, filling them with masonry, and heightened the building so that now it had a second floor.

Widdrington made other substantial improvements, yet preferred to live in their castle at Widdrington rather than in Haughton, and in a relatively short period of time the castle at Haughton became 'sadly neglected.'

The castle was restored by William Smith (using the services of John Dobson), in 1845.

Smith, nicknamed 'the Buccaneer' (no doubt because his wealth came from his maritime adventures), moved the main entrance to the north front, enclosed the park and diverted the road. He also removed the old village and established a wall-garden.

The Town Hall

The restoration work, carried out by John Dobson, was in keeping with the castle's ancient structures.

Tomlinson tells us that:

> 'the figure of the castle is that of a double square, with two parallel vaults of a simple construction running on the basement, from end to end.'

The walls of the castle are some eight feet thick and, in one part, eleven feet thick. Five square turrets crown the whole structure. In 1542 the castle was repaired after it was partly destroyed by Liddesdale raiders: John Dobson's restoration took place in 1845.

Photographed by kind permission of the owners (January, 1998).

The Town Hall *(North Shields)*

Standing as it does on Howard Street (Saville Street, to the right) this building, designed by John Dobson, 1844–45, it originally included police offices, a museum, savings bank and the Mechanics' Institute.

The Town Hall is now Council Offices and a Magistrates' Court.

The Town Hall, North Shields, Tyne and Wear

The Old Vicarage (now 'Longstone House') *(Chatton, Northumberland)*

The present 'Old Vicarage' (now known as 'Longstone House' and divided into two separate dwellings – East and West Longstone House – was built by John Dobson, in 1845, on the site of the former Vicarage House.

The Reverend Matthew Burrel, Vicar of Chatton at that time, had written to the Bishop of Durham (in whose Diocese the Vicarage lay), asking his permission to have the old Vicarage rebuilt.

He did not, however, receive either the Bishop's sympathetic support for his proposal or the response he had hopefully expected – far from it!

Edward, Bishop of Durham, wrote an 'Instrument' (dated the 4th of July, 1844) addressed to the Reverend Luke Yarcar (Vicar of Chillingham) and the Reverend Henry Parker (Rector of Ilderton). In it he expressed grave concerns about the situation at 'the Vicarage House at Chatton', and commissioned these two worthy clerics to 'make enquiry into the state and condition of the Buildings upon the Glebe, belonging to the said Benefice, at the time the said Matthew Burrell entered upon the same.'

The general tone of his 'Instrument' clearly illustrates the Bishop's deep misgivings and seems to suggest that perhaps all was not well at Chatton. The brief of the two appointed clergymen was quite explicit. The Bishop wanted to know 'as soon as conveniently may be', whether 'the said Matthew Burrell hath by wilful negligence suffered such buildings to go out of repair', and he further instructs that they must appraise him of 'the amount of the damage which such buildings have sustained by the wilful neglect of the said Matthew Burrell.' Strong language indeed!

Their eventual reply to the Bishop demonstrates that the two clergymen (Yarcar and Parker) had not only conducted a 'full enquiry' but that they had reached the same conclusion expressed, some four months later, by the architect John Dobson, that the Vicarage was in such a state of dilapidation as to be beyond repair. In Burrell's defence, however, they pointed out in their reply to the Bishop that he had only 'entered the said Living (i.e. Chatton) ... about the month of July, 1844' (so that, on the surface at least, it did seem rather unfair to blame the man for the state of a building which had suffered cruel neglect for many years previous to his occupancy).

The Reverend gentlemen also found that:

> 'the state of the building is extremely old and rudely built ... and of an inferior quality, the decay of which has been increased by the want of ventilation and proper drainage ...'

We also learn from their reply that Matthew Burrell was apparently to receive a sum of almost £105 'compensation' from the previous incumbent at Chatton 'for dilapidations' (a sum, we suppose, which was designed to help meet the costs of essential repairs to the building), but that this money had not been used for the purpose for which it was intended.

The Old Vicarage (now 'Longstone House'), Chatton, Northumberland

There are also 'law charges' mentioned in connection with the 'settlement' offered by the previous occupant but these are neither elaborated nor clarified.

Whatever mystery may or may not be attached to these disclosures, a mystery it must unfortunately remain, for there are no further papers available to 'lighten our darkness', as it were, and bring the story to a satisfactory conclusion. Sadly, we must remain in ignorance.

In any event, all of this information was duly relayed to the Bishop by The Reverend Yarcar and The Reverend Parker, in their reply of September 24th (1844), after an enquiry which had taken some three weeks to complete.

In a sworn affidavit, the following January (1845), John Dobson affirmed that he had examined the Vicarage at Chatton 'and finds that the whole is in such a state of dilapidation that it cannot be put into a habitable state of repair.' Mr Dobson then went on to justify his (professional) opinion with telling facts: 'The masonry ... is so bad that what can be got will scarcely repay the cost of pulling down the building and removing the rubbish ... the main timbers, flooring and other woodwork are in such a state of decay that no part can be used in the construction of a new building ... '

In a second affidavit (of January 16th, 1845), to the Reverend Luke Yarcar (who, as well as being Vicar of Chillingham, was also a Justice of the Peace), John Dobson declared that such, indeed, was the state of the old Vicarage House that old timber and other materials (doors, windows, boilers, etc) that might be

Longstone House, Chatton. The gable at the west end of the house has four steps, while, interestingly, the east gable has five

salvaged and were 'fit to be employed' in his proposed new building, had a value of only some £42-2-0.

Work began in 1845 and the estimate of expenses for the proposed new Vicarage (the present 'Longstone House') amounted, after deductions for useable old materials, to £1,453-16-3. John Dobson's own (architect's) fee was £70!

Designed by Dobson in 1845.

Photographed by kind permission of R. and H. K. Handyside, and Dr. and Mrs S. Spoor.

The Church of St Paul, Holme Eden, Warwick Bridge, Cumbria

The Church of St Paul *(Holme Eden, Warwick Bridge, Cumbria)*

Shortly after moving into Holme Eden, Peter Dixon (a devout Christian) offered to build and endow a church for the district. It was recognised that a new church was needed as the existing Parish Church (at Wetheral) could '... not afford accommodation for more than one third of the inhabitants'; so Dixon's offer was gladly accepted by the Diocese of Carlisle.

Peter Dixon provided the land for a church, churchyard and burial ground, met the cost of the building itself (said to have been about £1,500) and gave £2,500 (at 4% per annum) towards the stipend of the Vicar. The new church, dedicated in the name of St. Paul, together with the surrounding churchyard, was consecrated by Hugh Percy, Bishop of Carlisle, on Tuesday, September the 2nd, 1845.

The Church of St Paul was designed by John Dobson (and so, almost certainly, was the adjacent Vicarage).

Dobson's early training as a gardener gave him a special interest in the actual site of his buildings. It has been suggested that he almost preferred the landscape surrounding his works to the buildings themselves.

So it is easy to imagine that the beautiful site beside the River Eden that was put at his disposal for Holme Eden Church would have given him special pleasure.

Holme Eden Vicarage, Warwick Bridge, Cumbria

The exterior of the building is virtually unchanged from Dobson's original building. It is a very simple design in red sandstone with a slate roof and consists of a nave, a small chancel with an apse at the east end, a spire, 110 feet tall at the west end over the entrance porch and a small vestry at the south-east corner.

(I am obliged to the Rev. Stuart Casson, who very kindly placed his historical notes relating to St Paul's at my disposal).

Holme Eden Vicarage *(Warwick Bridge, Cumbria)*

Faulkner and Greg, in their book, *John Dobson, Newcastle Architect, 1787–1865*, written to commemorate the bi-centenary of Dobson's birth, ascribe to the Newcastle architect both the church and the vicarage – 'attributed on the grounds of style (Tudor) and proximity', but give the date as *c.*1836. As the church celebrated its centenary in 1945, this date (1836) would certainly appear to be incorrect.

Photographed by kind permission of Reverend J. S. Casson, of St Paul's Church, Warwick Bridge.

Holme Eden Vicarage, another view

Sandhoe House, Hexham, Northumberland

Sandhoe House *(Hexham, Northumberland)*

The house was built by John Dobson in 1850 for Sir Richard Errington. There is some argument as to whether the style is Tudor or Jacobean, but in any event Pevsner believes 'the house is not one of (Dobson's) best – although the porch is rather attractive.'

Even the date appears controversial, since the *Newcastle Daily Journal*, of January 16th, 1865, records 1843–45.

Photographed by kind permission of Mr J. Aidan Cuthbert.

The Baptist Church *(Howard Street, North Shields)*

'Dobson's Church' has three central windows above a moulded arch door. The gable is buttressed.

Described by the *Newcastle Daily Journal* as 'neo-Norman' the date is 1846.

The Baptist Church, Howard Street, North Shields, Tyne and Wear

Chollerton Grange, Chollerton, near Hexham, Northumberland

Chollerton Grange (Chollerton, near Hexham, Northumberland)

The plans for Dobson's (1847) alterations can be seen in the Northumberland County Records Office (Gosforth).

The (Old) Vicarage (Stamfordham, Northumberland)

The south side of the house consists of two sections.

The right section (two-storeyed) has four twelve-pane sash windows and a pedimented doorway containing a coat-of-arms.

The Vicarage lies immediately south of the church in a large walled garden ... considerable additions and alterations were made in 1762 by Dr Dockwray and there is some evidence that further alterations on the north side of the house were carried out by John Dobson about 1834.

Photographed by kind permission of Mr and Mrs I. Nicholson.

The (Old) Vicarage, Stamfordham, Northumberland

The Collingwood Monument, Tynemouth, Northumberland

The Collingwood Monument   *(Tynemouth, Northumberland)*

The monument is by John Dobson (1847): the twenty-three feet tall statue is by Lough: the cannon came from the *Royal Sovereign*.

The Collingwood Monument, another view, the large base has slit windows and a door

The (Castle) Keep, Newcastle upon Tyne

The (Castle) Keep   *(Newcastle upon Tyne)*

The Newcastle Daily Journal of January 16th, 1865 mentions that in 1847 John Dobson carried out (extensive) restorations of the Keep, 'paying particular attention to the Chapel and the entrance to the Great Hall'. Accommodation in the Hall soon became inadequate, however, and so, in 1855, the Society of Antiquaries accepted Dobson's proposed plan to provide more space.

    We are told that the necessary funds for such an enterprise were never forthcoming and so the architect's plans were unfortunately shelved.

    Photographed by kind permission of the Society of Antiquaries.

Church of St Cuthbert, Bensham Road, Gateshead
The church has a five-bay nave and a 'transitional tower' with a 'broach spire' (cf. St Cuthbert's, Benfieldside, Shotley Bridge). The west wall has triple windows under a single arch.

Church of St Cuthbert *(Bensham Road, Gateshead)*

A neo-Norman church by John Dobson (1845–48).

We are told St Cuthbert's was 'inspired by the 12th c. church at Barfreston, in Kent, which Dobson had examined in 1844.'

There have been additions to the church since it was built by John Dobson and it is now some years since it was used as a place of worship (1999); indeed, the future of St Cuthbert's is extremely uncertain.

Church of St Cuthbert, Bensham Road, Gateshead
The carved 'chancel' arch is like that in St Andrew's Church, Newcastle, which Dobson had restored in 1844.

Church of St Mary the Virgin   *(Stamfordham, Northumberland)*

A church has stood here since at least the beginning of the 13th c. and quite probably before that time.

The present building was almost entirely rebuilt in 1848–9 under the direction of the architect, Benjamin Ferrey, and it was during the time of these repairs and restorations that John Dobson was involved (1848).

Church of St Mary the Virgin, Stamfordham, Northumberland

St John's Church *(Grainger Street/Westgate Road, Newcastle upon Tyne)*

The Newcastle Courant (July 2nd, 1848) states that John Dobson carried out restoration work, in 1848. The west tower is believed to be 15th c. and has 'quite elaborate pinnacles'.

Welton
(Horsley-on-the-Hill, Northumberland)

The small Keeper's Cottage with its stepped gable and sets of tripartite windows is on the left. The more imposing Directors' Meeting Rooms are on the right.

Above: *The Keeper's Cottage, Welton*

Left: *The Keeper's Cottage. Horsley-on-the-Hill, Northumberland. This octagonal tower (designed by John Dobson) was the Directors' Meeting Room.*

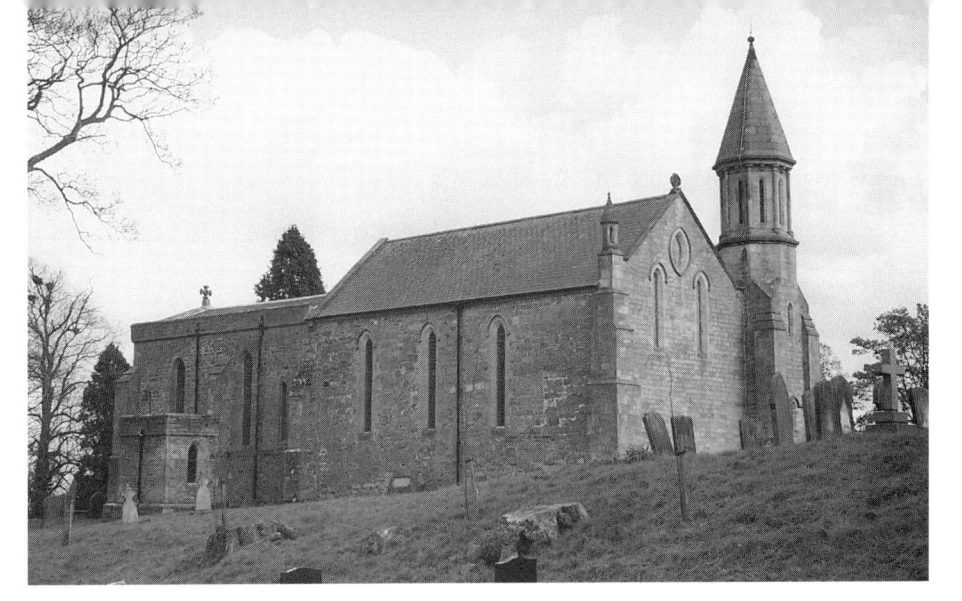

The Church of St Andrew, Winston on Tees, County Durham

Church of St Andrew *(Winston on Tees, County Durham)*

The exterior of the church was rebuilt by John Dobson in 1848.

All Saints Church *(Fulwell Road, Monkwearmouth, Sunderland, Co. Durham)*

A church by John Dobson: 1845–49.

It is small, in the Early English style and, as one writer puts it, 'an excellent effect is achieved by simple means.'

All Saints Church, Fulwell Road, Monkwearmouth, Sunderland, Co. Durham

Period V 1840–50

The Church of St John the Baptist *(Meldon, Northumberland)*

Described as a small but attractive building, consecrated in the 13 c. John Dobson carried out some restoration work on St John's in 1849.

The Church of St John the Baptist, Meldon, Northumberland

The Church of St Peter, Bywell, Northumberland

The Church of St Peter (Bywell, Northumberland)

The architecture covers many centuries.

The nave is considered to be early Norman: three round-headed windows in the north wall may well be even earlier. The remainder of the church is essentially 13th c., though the three lancet windows behind the altar are Early English and the north chapel was added in the fourteenth century.

Above: The south porch (in the photograph) was added in the 19th c.

M. J. Dobson, in her *Memoir*, claims her father carried out restoration work on St Peter's in 1849.

Central Station, Newcastle upon Tyne

Central Station *(Newcastle upon Tyne)*

'The Central Station was opened by Queen Victoria and Prince Albert on August 29th, 1850.

The day was declared a public holiday and local manufacturers were asked to put their fires out between eleven o'clock in the morning and two in the afternoon, so as not to cloud the momentous occasion.

Local legend has it that this was Victoria's last visit to Newcastle.

After the celebration banquet, the manager of the hotel (?) had the cheek to present the Queen with the bill!

In future, whenever she passed through the town, the blinds were always pulled down in her carriage.

(Ref. *Newcastle upon Tyne: Northern Heritage*, p. 113).

'The iron-worked roofing was unique at the time. Dobson devised a process which pressed the iron out between the rollers instead of cutting it from flattened plates (the work was provided by Hawk, Crawley & Co., of Gateshead) and Dobson's invention (now universally copied) won him a prize at the Paris Exposition.'

(Ref. *Newcastle upon Tyne: Northern Heritage*).

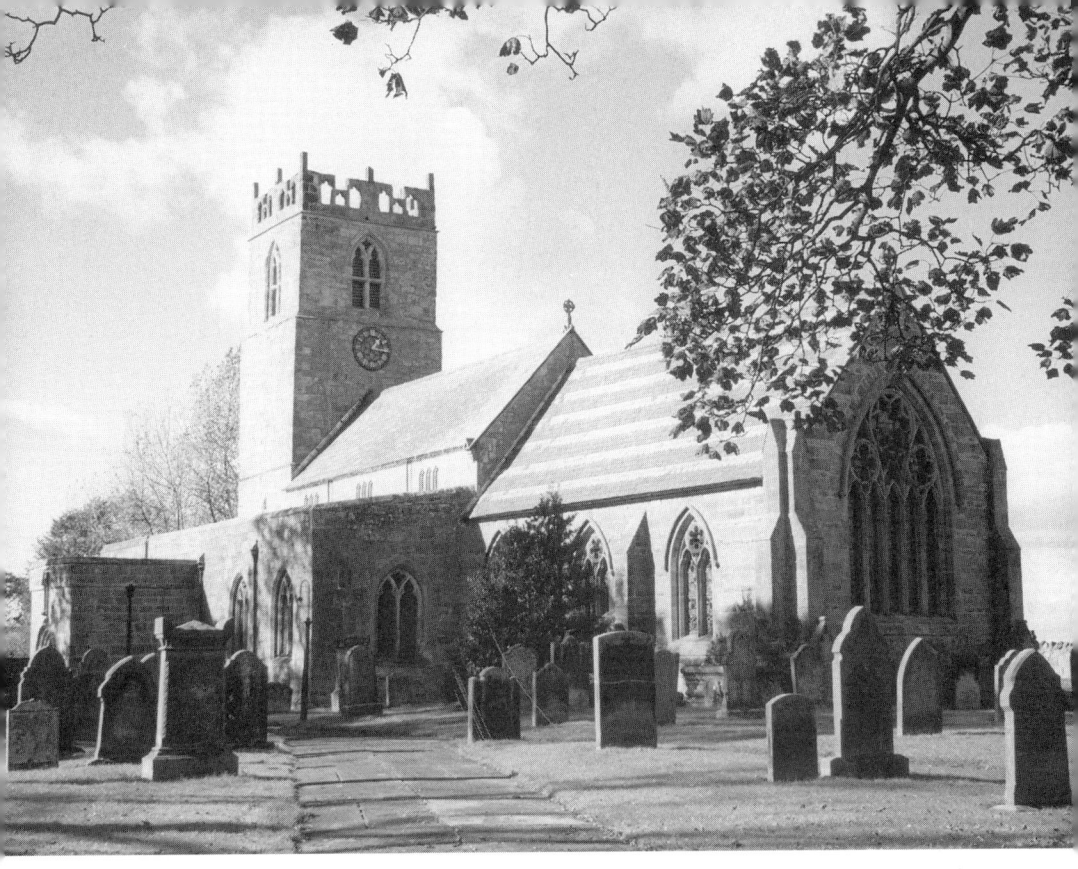

Church of the Holy Trinity, Embleton, near Alnwick, Northumberland

Church of the Holy Trinity (Embleton, near Alnwick, Northumberland)

The nave aisles were extended westward as far as the west wall of the tower, so that the latter was incorporated in the body of the church. The extension of the north aisle became the Grey porch or family pew. The Vincent Edwards and Grey galleries were presumably demolished at this time.

All the windows were replaced by ones with 19th c. decorated tracery. The nave roof was renewed but the aisle roofs were left as they were (apart from some strengthening of the southern one).

The Craster porch was taken down and rebuilt on the same foundations, but higher than before.

(Ref. *A History of Embleton Church*, by Oswin Craster).

Above: As well as the work mentioned above, John Dobson also inserted a ceiling in the lower portion of the tower, supported by stone arches. The restoration work was carried out by Dobson in 1849–50.

Church of St Cuthbert, Benfieldside, Shotley Bridge, Co. Durham

The Church of St Andrew, Bywell, near Stocksfield, Northumberland

Church of St Cuthbert (Benfieldside, Shotley Bridge, Co. Durham)

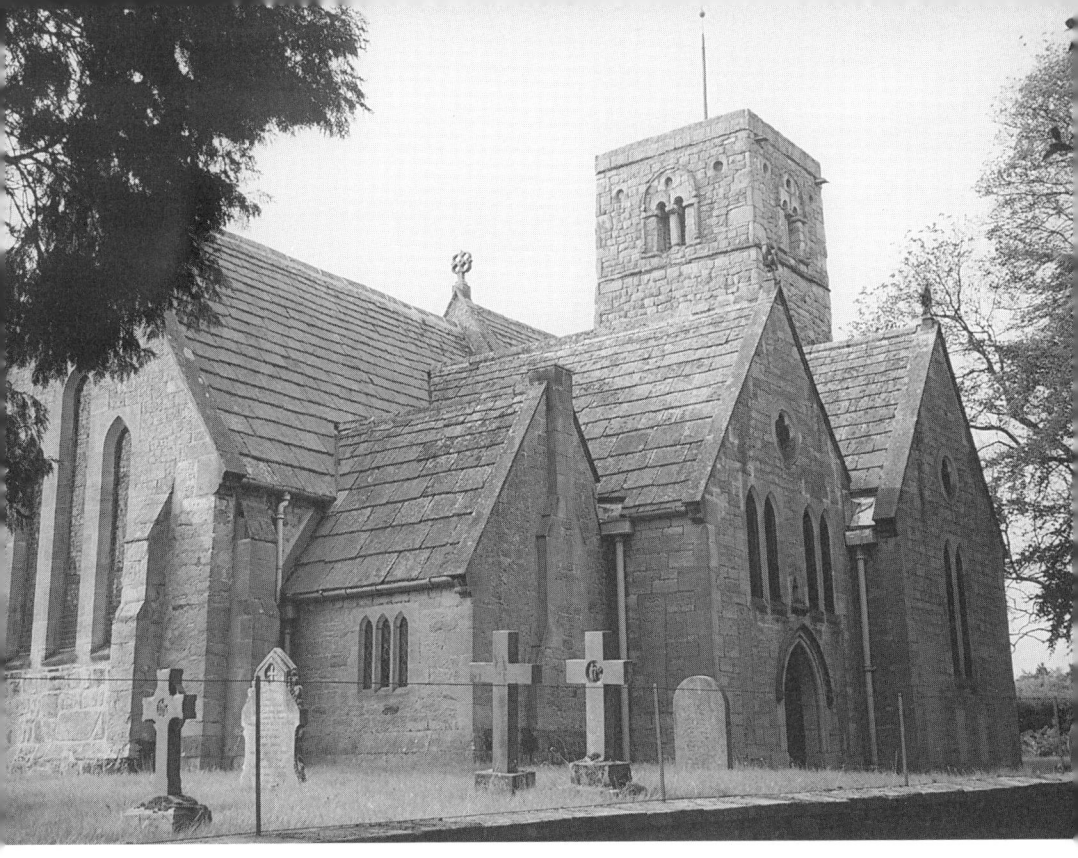

Opposite: The church, by John Dobson (1849–50), is in the Early English style. The tower has a 'broach spire', like that on St Cuthbert's Church on Bensham Road, Gateshead, another of Dobson's churches.

The Church of St Andrew (Bywell, near Stocksfield, Northumberland)

Tradition has it that St Wilfred built a (Saxon) church on this site, in the seventh century. Its imposing pre-Norman tower shows signs of both Saxon characteristics and Roman materials used in its construction. W. W. Tomlinson writes that 'on June 11th, 803, Egbert, the twelfth Bishop of Lindisfarne, was consecrated here by Archbishop Eanbald.' The church was altered in 1830, and again in 1850, by John Dobson.

Above: The pre-Conquest Tower and South Porch.

St Andrew's was known as 'the White Church' from the white canons of Blanchland, to whom it belonged, and St Peter's 'the Black Church' from the black Benedictine monks of Durham.

PERIOD VI
1851–65

The Barber Surgeons' Hall, Victoria Street, Newcastle upon Tyne

The Barber Surgeons' Hall   *(Victoria Street, Newcastle upon Tyne)*

Wilkes declares John Dobson designed the ('Italianate') Surgeons' Hall in 1851.

Almshouses   *(Hospital of St Mary the Virgin, Rye Hill, Newcastle upon Tyne)*

Following enquiries into the affairs of the charity by the Court of Chancery in both 1840 and 1846, an Act of Parliament was passed for the erection of the new Almshouses and a Chapel.

Sir George Rose (Master in Chancery) threw open to competition the designs and plans for the building of the new church, almshouses and hospital at Rye Hill.

Almshouses, Hospital of St Mary the Virgin, Rye Hill, Newcastle upon Tyne

Period VI 1851–65

The (Royal) Station Hotel, Neville Street, Newcastle upon Tyne

A number of tenders were thereupon exhibited, for public appraisal, in the Merchants' Court, Guildhall.

'After an examination of all the plans, the meeting (of proprietors of property in Elswick) came to a unanimous conclusion of forwarding a memorial recommending the plans submitted by Mr Dobson – *in which conclusion we (i.e. the Local Commissioners) entirely concur.*'

(Ref. *The Newcastle Chronicle*: August 22nd, 1851.)

Photographed by kind permission of Mr David Watson: Administrator.

The (Royal) Station Hotel *(Neville Street, Newcastle upon Tyne)*

Described simply as 'classical, 1851', in the *Newcastle Courant* of July 11th, 1851, Neville Street (according to the *Newcastle Daily Journal* of 16th January, 1865) had

The (Royal) Station Hotel, Neville Street, Newcastle upon Tyne

been planned by John Dobson in 1828 and built around 1835. The Hotel was built in 1851.

> 'Dobson's stone four-storey hotel had reception rooms on the ground floor, grand suites with high ceilings on the first floor, and smaller rooms above – one hundred bedrooms in all, for families and single people.
>
> His building is now less than a quarter of the present hotel, recognisable as the ten-bay, four-storey section closer to the station ...
>
> The window-head pattern on Dobson's first floor is continued across the (1890) extension.'

(Ref. *The Buildings of Grainger Town. Four Townscape Walks around Newcastle*: pp. 64/5 David Lovie (English Partnership). Photographed by kind permission of Mr Arvin Handa.

Benfieldside Vicarage (St Cuthbert's: Shotley Bridge, Co. Durham)

The church of St Cuthbert was built (by John Dobson) between 1849–50.

Following Pages: A Dobson building in the Tudor style, 1851; according to the *Newcastle Journal*, 11th January, 1851.

Photographed by kind permission of the Reverend Martin Jackson, Vicar of St Cuthbert's.

The Vicar also believes his to be a Dobson building of about the same period as the church 'on the grounds of proximity and style.'

Benfieldside Vicarage, St Cuthbert's: Shotley Bridge, Co. Durham

Newton Hall, now Mowden Hall School, Newton, Stocksfield

Newton Hall (*now Mowden Hall School, Newton, Stocksfield*)

The original building (as Newton Hall) is dated 1811.

John Dobson made additions and alterations in 1851. The south front had five bays; the pedimented centrepiece was added later. W. H. Blackett commissioned John Dobson to carry out alterations in 1851. Since the end of the last War, the Hall has been adapted for use as a school and it is now 'Mowden Hall School', Newton, near Stocksfield.

Photographed by kind permission of Mr A. P. Lewis (Headmaster).

Newton Hall, now Mowden Hall School, Newton, Stocksfield

The Percy Chapel, Tynemouth (Priory), Northumberland, with the Priory behind

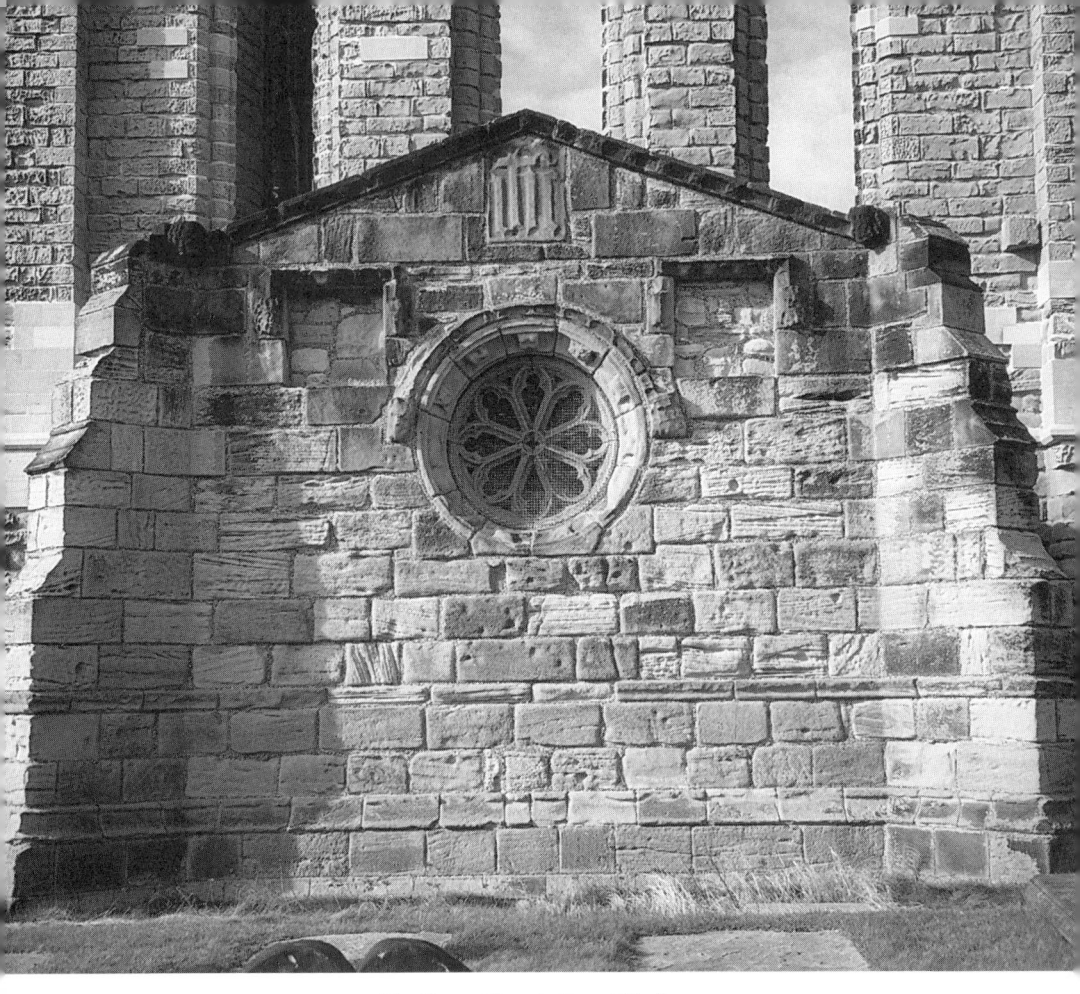

The Percy Chapel, Rose Window

The Percy Chapel   *(Tynemouth (Priory), Northumberland)*

The Newcastle Chronicle of 27th of August, 1852 tells that John Dobson carried out restoration work on the Chapel, in 1852.

> 'The Chapel has a vaulted roof with curiously intersecting ribs terminating in three bosses (i.e. 'knobs' or 'studs', 'raised ornaments'), adorned with figures of the Saviour, the Virgin Mary and the Twelve Apostles, which are surrounded by legends now nearly effaced.
>
> Several heraldic bearings of the Percy family are sculptured in this chapel and the arms of the Delaval family also can still be seen on the inside of the door.'

(Ref. W. W. Tomlinson's *Comprehensive Guide to Northumberland*.)

Photographed by kind permission of English Heritage.

The Leazes, Hexham, Northumberland

The Leazes *(Hexham, Northumberland)*

'The Leazes is situated in the heart of Northumberland, one mile west of the busy market town of Hexham.

The word 'Leazes' means 'the meadow'. Locally, however, it has two other names: 'Myln Care' (because of a road that once passed the Leazes to some old Chimney Mills) and 'Blind Man's Loaning' (because an old beggar was reputed to have sat frequently outside the house).

John Dobson redesigned Leazes for a landed gentry family on a scale which created an impressive piece of architecture, and it blended into its environment.

John Drayton (architect) said that mansions of Dobson's designs were always considered an element *in* that environment and not an isolated piece of architecture.

In 1842 the Leazes was bought by James Gibson, one of the wealthiest landowners in the area, who subsequently changed his name to Kirsopp.

Oddly enough, James Kirsopp never lived at the Leazes: it was never more than a building on land that he owned.

In 1851 William Kirsopp bought the Leazes. He commissioned John Dobson to carry out extensive alterations to the house. A comprehensive rebuilding and enlargement programme began under the supervision of John Dobson. The date of the construction of the earlier part of the Leazes is unknown, as are the names of the architects and builders.

The Leazes, Hexham, Northumberland

The earliest document concerning work done at the Leazes dates from 1851, when a letter asked Dobson to alter and enlarge the house. The earliest and only plans so far located are of the stables, piggeries, cart sheds and byres, and these are dated 1905.

Examination of these plans will reveal the initial size and shape of the house (plans for proposed buildings did not require planning permission before 1880). It is, however, reasonably possible to speculate on the date of the original construction of the Leazes by referring to other houses in the area built of the same stone and with a known date of construction. This may have been 1840, more than ten years before its reconstruction. The alterations were extensive; more than three-quarters of the house was rebuilt.

The vagaries of the weather were always an important consideration in Dobson's thinking and planning, and protection from the cold north wind was always a priority. In the case of the Leazes, he built the main entrance on the south-east corner, sheltered both from the north wind and the prevailing westerlies. The passage of cold currents of air (draughts!) is further restricted by the addition of a porch at the main entrance and then by double doors and passageways throughout. According to Dobson, this was to trap the air.

Dampness below the floors was overcome by placing a 'vent' in the wall on a level with the surface of the ground, which allowed a thorough ventilation throughout the building. After adopting this plan, he apparently never knew an instance of 'dry rot'.

The Leazes, another view

This 'vent' has also been called a 'dry drain' and has now become a common and expedient feature of building work. Yet this somewhat small 'discovery' by Dobson was considered an extremely important 'invention' at the time. His assiduous attention to small detail was commendable, but then, as Dobson himself said, 'We build houses to live in not just to look at: we need to do our utmost to encourage the useful, as the beautiful will take care of itself.'

Dobson's external elevations for the Leazes show a segmented front divided into three narrow faces, across the top of which are triangular pediments, successfully exaggerating the height of the building. Another factor designed to give the impression of height is the actual design of the windows. John Dobson, like others of his contemporaries, appreciated the importance and dignity created by over-tall windows (their height being something in the order of three times their width).

The surrounding of the windows is plain and clean-cut, designed to enhance their simplicity.

The bay windows (in the west wing, for example) are also a regular feature of Dobson's country houses, *their* primary purpose being to afford panoramic (and often breathtaking) views of the surrounding countryside.

Nothing was allowed to interfere with the purity of Dobson's designs for country houses.

Here, as in other Dobson houses, the drainpipes and plumbing were installed internally so that no sight of them showed on the outer face of the building. In the recent conversions to the Leazes this has had to be altered, as obviously new plumbing and drainage had to be installed on existing structures.

The house was re-built and enlarged for William Kirsopp in 1850 by John Dobson.

The 'bay' on the left of the building is a later addition to Dobson's house.

Photographed by kind permission of Mr John Knipe and Dr George Ward.

I must acknowledge Carol Ward's sources of information as, indirectly, they are mine also:

Lyall Wilkes, both in personal correspondence and in Lyall Wilkes and Gordon Dodds, *Tyneside Classical*.

Andrew Jackson Downing, *The Architecture of Country Houses 1816–52*.

Mark Girouard, *Life in the English Country House*.

Jill Franklin, *The Gentleman's Country House, 1835–1914*.

Marian Page, *Historic Houses Restored and Preserved*.

Frank Graham, *Historic Newcastle*.

Nikolaus Pevsner and Pevsner and Richmond, *The Buildings of England: Northumberland*, 1957 and 1992 Editions.

Margaret Jane Dobson, *A Memoir of John Dobson*.

Also I am obliged to J. V. Welch, Chartered Surveyor, for his assistance in researching into the construction of the Leazes, and those people who once lived and worked in the Leazes for any information they may kindly have been able to supply.

Church of St Michael and All Angels (Ford, Northumberland)

This lovely thirteenth-century church was standing here, overlooking the Cheviot Hills, before the castle was even built. It has, we are told, one feature which is 'archaeologically as interesting as it is architecturally successful': its bellcote.

John Dobson carried out extensive restoration work on this church in 1853–54. He was commissioned to 'modernise' the church and restore it to its basic thirteenth-century character. This he did to a remarkable degree and extremely successfully, even though Pevsner accuses him of 'over-restoring' it. He enlarged the chancel arch and redesigned the chancel itself. He added the north aisle, heightened the roof of the nave by some eight feet and added the south entrance porch. The windows throughout the church were redesigned and 'an old lancet in the west wall, which had been blocked up, was restored. It is now fitted with a stained glass window of St. Michael.' Dobson added the south entrance porch in 1853–4.

The outside of the building is as fascinating as the interior. All the windows, which were remodelled by him in 1854, have simple hood moulds, each of which bears two stone carved faces. The *Church Notes* remark that 'It is difficult to say whether these were the work of nineteenth-century stonemasons, or whether they were old stones from some other building, re-used in this charming way ... '

Church of St Michael and All Angels, Ford, Northumberland

Church of St Michael and All Angels, Ford, Northumberland

Church of St Michael and All Angels, Ford, Northumberland, showing the bellcote and the south porch

Period VI 1851–65

Left: *Church of St Michael and All Angels, Ford, Northumberland. Window with moulding showing two carved faces*

Below: *Church of St Michael and All Angels, Ford, Northumberland, interior view.*

Yet while W. W. Tomlinson (*Comprehensive Guide to Northumberland*, p. 522) agrees that '... the work was executed with such good taste that the antique charm of the building has not been destroyed'. P. Anderson Graham (*Highways and Byways in Northumbria*, p. 71) complains that '... restoration and improvement have obliterated many of the most interesting features'.

Church of St Mary *(Gateshead-on-Tyne)*

The Parish Church has twice been severly damaged by fire – firstly in the 'Great Fire' which began on October 6th, 1854, and, again, in 1979.

> 'The restoration of the Parish Church of St. Mary (Gateshead), which suffered so severely by the explosion (of 1854) was ... entrusted to Mr Dobson, and its completion was such as to call forth the approbation of the Bishop of the Diocese.'

(Ref. *The Newcastle Daily Journal*, January 9th, 1865).

The (Castle) Keep, Newcastle upon Tyne

The (Castle) Keep (Newcastle upon Tyne)

The battlements were all restored by John Dobson in 1847.

Following Pages: In 1847 considerable restoration was carried out by John Dobson. His proposed plan of 1855 to organise more exhibition space, while accepted, was eventually shelved through lack of funds. Photographed by kind permission of The Society of Antiquaries.

The (Castle) Keep, Newcastle upon Tyne

Period VI 1851–65

St John's Church, Grainger Street/Westgate Road, Newcastle upon Tyne

St John's Church *(Grainger Street/Westgate Road, Newcastle upon Tyne)*

A Parish Church of the 13th c. which was altered considerably in the 15th c. Described as 'an oasis among modern buildings ... '. Grey called it 'a pretty little church ... because it much resembles a cross.'

John Dobson refitted the chancel in 1855.

Wallington Hall *(Cambo, Morpeth, Northumberland)*

In medieval times there was a castle at Wallington. In the middle of the 16th c. the Fenwicks added a Tudor house to the castle (cellars of the present building contain the original foundations). Sir William Blackett, a rich Newcastle businessman, bought Wallington in 1684. He demolished the Fenwicks' Tudor house and four years later began to build the house which stands (its exterior almost unchanged) today.

Wallington Hall, Cambo, Morpeth, Northumberland. The east front is beautifully symmetrical in its appearance. Two storeys with eleven bays. The two bays at either end project slightly. The single bay centre also projects. It has quoins and the doorway has two Tuscan columns and a pediment. The Hall is built of honey-coloured sandstone and had a hipped roof.

Wallington Hall, Cambo, Morpeth, Northumberland. The south front has nine bays with a three-bay, slightly projecting, centrepiece with pediment. It too has quoins.

Wallington Hall: Picture Gallery

Wallington Hall: Picture Gallery.

Photographed by kind permission of the National Trust.

Holy Trinity Vicarage *(Seghill, Northumberland)*

The Tudor-style Vicarage is attributed to John Dobson – 1855.
   Photographed by kind permission of Mr Colin Lawson.

Holy Trinity Vicarage, Seghill, Northumberland

St John's Church, Otterburn, Northumberland

St John's Church (Otterburn, Northumberland)

Tomlinson tells us that the church, built after designs by John Dobson and dedicated to St John the Baptist, was opened in 1857.

It is, says Tomlinson, a handsome stone building in the Decorated style and contains some fine memorial windows.

St Columba's Presbyterian Church (North Shields)

Designed by John Dobson (1856-57) and built in the Palladian style. It has five arched bays with Tuscan half-columns.

It is now a United Reformed Church.

St Columba's Presbyterian Church, North Shields

Chatton Bridge, Chatton, Northumberland

Chatton Bridge (Chatton, Northumberland)

The 'Bridge on the Fell' is an early 18 c. construction.

It lies on the B6348 road from Wooler to Belford, a quarter of a mile or so east of the village of Chatton, across the River Till.

The bridge has three segmental arches and triangular cutaways. Originally it was some ten feet wide but in 1857 the arches were doubled in thickness by John Dobson.

Chatton Bridge, Chatton, Northumberland. The lower of the two photographs shows where Dobson doubled the 'thickness' of the bridge in 1857

The Mechanics' Institute, Howard Street/Saville Street, North Shields

The Mechanics' Institute *(Howard Street/Saville Street, North Shields)*

This lovely building was designed by John Johnstone in 1857–58. In 1869 it became a Public (Free) Library and in 1974 the North Shields Local Studies Centre.

Since 1994 it has been the North Tyneside Business Centre.

Described as 'Italianate', the building is of red brick with stucco trim. In the 1992 edition of *The Building of England: Northumberland*, we are told John Dobson *may* have made alterations to the building – but no date is given.

Hexham Abbey *(Hexham, Northumberland)*

Following Page: The east front (looking onto the Market Place) replaced a medieval east end. First altered by John Dobson in 1828, it was finally replaced by him (not without considerable controversy) in 1858. It is said to be modelled on Whitby Abbey.

Hexham Abbey, Hexham, Northumberland, the east front

Holeyn Hall, Wylam, Northumberland

Holeyn Hall (Wylam, Northumberland)

A Georgian house with balustraded six-bay south front and three-storeyed balustraded tower. The tower is 'attached' to the earlier 18th c. house. The balustraded south front with the square tower is John Dobson's work of 1858.

Dobson made large additions to the Hall for Edward James in 1858.

Holeyn Hall, Wylam, Northumberland

Holeyn Hall, Wylam, Northumberland. East front, also balustraded.

Dr Frank Atkinson describes the Hall as 'a country house of 1851, with additions by John Dobson in 1858.'

Photographed by kind permission of Dr and Mrs John Williams and Drs W. and A. Brough.

Shawdon Hall *(Glanton, Alnwick, Northumberland)*

James Hargreaves (solicitor) was High Sheriff of Northumberland in 1738. When he died, he left the Hall to his sister Mary, who married John Pawson. This John Pawson's grandson inherited the house and the estate in 1817. The Pawsons were wealthy landowners but rather too fond of gambling on both horses and greyhounds (coursing).

The story has it that if one of their horses lost a race which it had been confidently expected to win, the unfortunate animal was returned to the stable-yard, shot, and its carcass dumped in a bog on the estate. The same thing, apparently, happened to a dog whose performance failed to match its master's expectations.

Eventually, and perhaps not surprisingly, the Pawsons went bankrupt and the estate had to be sold.

There has been a house at Shawdon ever since the thirteenth century. Hodgson (*History of Northumberland*) tells us : 'William of Glanton sold land at

Shawdon Hall, Glanton, Alnwick, Northumberland

Shawdon Hall, Glanton, Alnwick, Northumberland. The two-storeyed, seven-bay south front with decorated central pediment on four pilasters. The Hall is said to stand on the site of an old pele-tower.

Period VI 1851–65

Shawdon to John de la Green and William's widow, Joan, claimed possession of a dower, in 1296.'

Additions and alterations to Shawdon Hall were made by John Dobson, in 1825. Further alterations were made in 1858 for John Pawson.

Shawdon Hall. Flight of steps leading up to a central Venetian doorway

Shawdon Hall. A gate lodge

Both gate lodges are mid 19th c. and probably by Dobson. Photographed by kind permission of Major R. F. Cowan.

Church of St Paul *(High Elswick, Newcastle upon Tyne)*

John Dobson's work was often impaired by a shortage of money. He complained that he had been unable to make the exterior of St Paul's (one of his largest churches) as attractive as he would have liked for this reason.

The style is Gothic and the church was built in 1857, being consecrated in 1858. St Paul's is now the only Christian denominational place of worship in the parish. For many years the Church Hall has been a Community Centre.

Church of St Paul, High Elswick, Newcastle upon Tyne

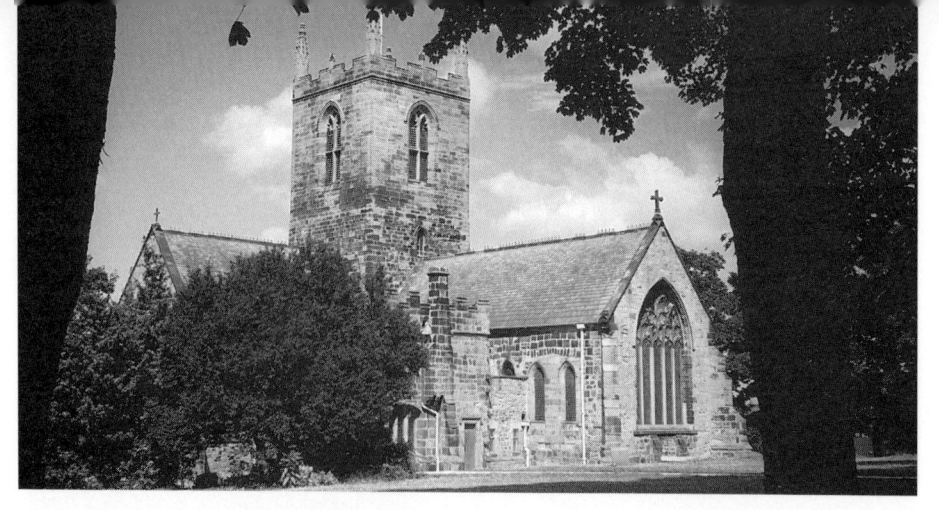

The Parish Church of St Michael and All Angels, Houghton-le-Spring, Co. Durham

The Parish Church of St Michael and All Angels   *(Houghton-le-Spring, Co. Durham)*

Margaret Jane Dobson, in her *Memoir* of 1885, gives us the following detailed account of the restoration work her father carried out at St Michael's in 1859.

> 'As another proof of Mr Dobson's inventive skill, the work that he did at the fine old Norman church of St Michael's ... may be cited. About the year 1828, a tower to contain a peal of six bells had been added, which weighed about 1500 tons. This enormous mass of masonry caused the pillars on the north-east and the south-east of the tower to shrink, as they had not originally been constructed to carry such pressure, added to which the foundations also were becoming seriously weakened by the formation of vaults.
>
> In 1859 Mr Dobson undertook the arduous and difficult task of taking out the pillars and replacing them by new ones. This he ingeniously accomplished by carrying the solid mass of the superincumbent masonry on wooden centres; and to make the work more secure, he

The Parish Church of St Michael and All Angels, Houghton-le-Spring, Co. Durham. Another view

Cathedral Church of St Nicholas, Newcastle upon Tyne, the east gate

had the whole of the debris within the tower taken out to the depth of the foundations, and the space solidly filled in with concrete, thus preventing any external pressure from the ground outside which was so much above the foundations. The whole of this work was accomplished without any shrinking or settlement of the structure.

We are told by Mr J. W. A. Robinson, who was Churchwarden at the time, that Mr Dobson, with his usual liberality, presented his professional fee towards the church restoration fund.'

A Norman Church once existed on the site of the present building but most of the present church is 13th c.

Cathedral Church of St Nicholas (Newcastle upon Tyne)

In 1824 John Dobson rebuilt the north end of the north transept and in 1859 the east wall. In both cases he altered the windows ...

In *Archaelogia Aeliana* (4th series): Vol. IX, Honeyman confirms that Dobson rebuilt the east gable in 1859 'with a single enormous window instead of the two it originally held.'

Period VI 1851–65

Church of St John the Baptist *(Grainger Street/Wastgate Road, Newcastle)*

According to Margaret Jane Dobson (*Memoir*, p. 104), her father designed the altar railings and the reredos for St John's in 1859.

Church of St John the Baptist, Grainger Street/Wastgate Road,

Unthank Hall, facing south, near Haltwhistle, Northumberland

Unthank Hall *(near Haltwhistle, Northumberland)*

The house was remodelled in 1815 and again in 1860 (though there is some dispute regarding the second date), both times by John Dobson. The bulk of the Hall is late 19th c. The right side of the building (in the photograph) is most probably part of Dobson's work.

Unthank Hall, west end.

This is the part of the Hall, with its mullioned tripartite windows, where Dobson is believed to have made his alterations. Photographed by kind permission of Mr and Mrs W. R. Webster.

Church of St Lawrence, Warkworth, Northumberland

Church of St Lawrence (Warkworth, Northumberland)

Described as a large and fairly complete Norman Church (erected on the site of the Saxon Church of King Ceolwulf) and 'unique in Northumberland'. Remains of this earlier church were discovered during restoration work in 1860, when John Dobson restored both the nave and chancel. The tower is believed to have been added *c.* 1200.

Church of St Gregory (Kirknewton, Northumberland)

The Church of St Gregory, which was rebuilt in the time of Charles II (*c.* 1670)

Church of St Gregory, Kirknewton, Northumberland

Church of St Gregory, Kirknewton, Northumberland

and was restored by Dobson in 1860, stands on the site of a Norman edifice. The base of a Norman buttress and part of the foundations of the early building were laid bare by Mr F. R. Wilson during some excavations in 1857.

The chancel is a very remarkable one, being, it is supposed, the vaulted chamber of a pele or store house built out of the ruins of the Norman church. Built up in the wall of the tower on the outside is a child's coffin lid with a florinated cross upon it.

Attached to the wall behind the reading desk is a curious piece of sculpture representing the Virgin and the Magi – the Wise men appear, incongruously, in kilts!

(Ref. W. W. Tomlinson's *Comprehensive Guide to Northumberland*, p. 506).

In 1860 John Dobson rebuilt the nave and north aisle, though at the time there was considerable opposition to his plan.

Jesmond Parish Church (Jesmond, Newcastle upon Tyne)

A late Early English Church with big, pinnacled tower. Designed by John Dobson, 1857–61.

Designed by John Dobson and built in memory of Richard Clayton. It is also known as the Clayton Memorial Church.

Jesmond Parish Church, Jesmond, Newcastle upon Tyne

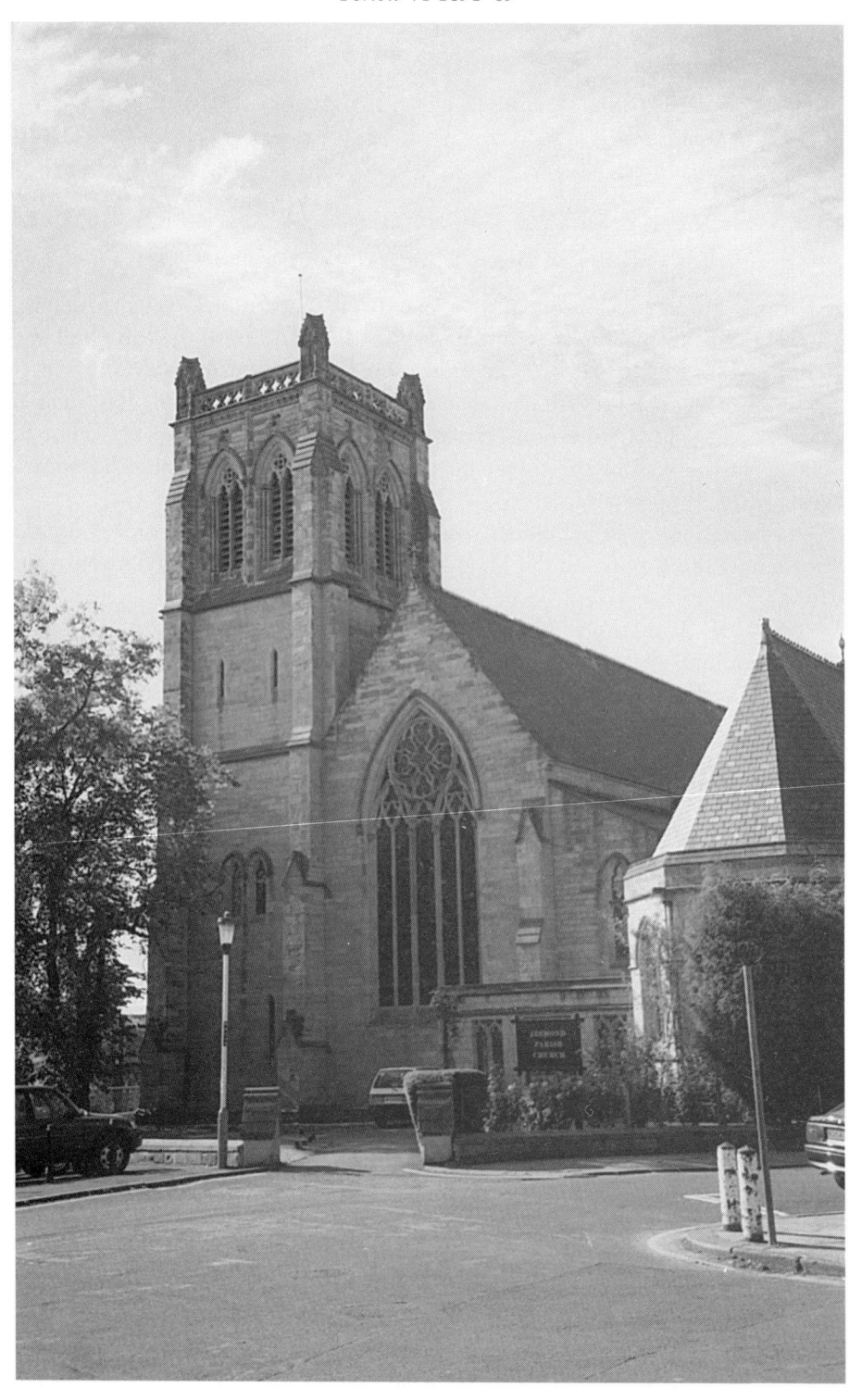

Period VI 1851–65

Jesmond Parish Church, Jesmond, Newcastle upon Tyne

Lambton Castle *(Chester-le-Street, County Durham)*

Many of Lambton Castle's problems in the middle the 19th c. stemmed from the fact that the castle was built over forgotten mine-workings.

The castle had been enlarged by Ignatius Bonomi in the 1820s, but by 1854 the building showed distinct signs of imminent collapse. In short it was 'almost wrecked by subsidence.'

It is perhaps the ultimate compliment to John Dobson's talents as an engineer (write Faulkner and Greg) that he should have been called in in 1857, at the age of 69, to underpin the castle and to design major new extensions to it.

Dobson (also) designed new reception rooms around a Great Hall.

'A picturesque house, which is the product of several re-buildings, the first between 1798 and 1801 by Joseph Bonomi, and later, in 1862, by Sydney Smirke and John Dobson.
   In the 1930s the house was reduced in size.'

(Ref. *Historic Architecture of County Durham*, p. 55, Neville Whittaker and Ursula Clark).

Lambton Castle, Chester-le-Street, County Durham

Lambton Castle. An octagonal tower with splayed base

Lambton Castle. North side and west front with porte-cochère

The Lamb Bridge

Bonomi's magnificent 'Lamb Bridge', with a span of some 82 feet (c. 24½ metres): there are lambs on the abutments. Photographed by kind permission of the Lambton Estate (Mr Robert Kirton-Darling, Estate Manager).

Period VI 1851–65

When, by the mid-1850s, the castle was in imminent danger of collapse, Ignatius Bonomi was made the scapegoat. His 'bad' designs were blamed for the castle's problems when, in fact, it was because it had been built on disused mine-workings, which was the real cause of the problem.

The task of 'shoring up the building' was given to John Dobson and his son-in-law, Sydney Smirke, and a small fortune was spent filling up the old seams and stabilising the foundations.

Central Station *(Newcastle upon Tyne)*

Although the Station, with its portico, is a fine building, it falls well short of what John Dobson intended.

His colonnaded front was rejected as was his Italianate tower and even the portico was not at first accepted (built eventually by Prosser, in 1863, only two years before Dobson's death).

The original (1848) portico design was truly a work of art; it has been described as 'equal to Vanbrugh's grandest designs and, if executed, will be the finest thing of its kind in Europe. Newcastle may be proud of its architect.'

Central Station (Newcastle upon Tyne)

Central Station

John Dobson's Death

In 1859, at the age of 72, John Dobson was elected first President of the newly formed Northern Architectural Association.

He retired from active work in 1863 when he suffered a stroke, which left him partly paralysed and from which he never really recovered. He kept on his house in New Bridge Street but moved to a house at Ryton, where, it was hoped, the country air and surroundings would benefit his health.

At the end of December, 1864 he was weakening and returned with his daughter to 15, New Bridge Street, where he died on Sunday, January 8th, 1865, leaving two sons and two daughters.

He also left 'a comfortable fortune' of just under £16,000.

The Newcastle Daily Chronicle of January 9th, 1865 referred to his outstanding contribution to the architecture of the North and his:

> 'robust, powerful frame which enabled him in after years to do the work of three ordinary men, and a hearty, genial temper and straightforward honesty of conduct which cleared his professional course of many obstacles and made many friends of all he came in contact; few men (*The Chronicle* added) have spent so long a life in so laborious a manner and made so few enemies.'

Dobson's passing was not, however, felt to mark the end of an era in Newcastle, nor felt in the profound way in which Grainger's was. So much of Dobson's work had been spread throughout Northumberland and Durham ... on the designing of country homes.

Dobson had always been a quiet and retiring, professional man and had never become (and would have hated to become) the ebullient public figure which Grainger had been.

(Ref. *Tyneside Classical*, p. 114, Wilkes and Dodds).

Opposite Top: John Dobson's grave (with marble headstone) in the cemetery he designed.

It speaks volumes for the 'area of his birth' that (in 1997) the site of his birth is a public house in Chirton, North Shields, which is boarded up and covered in graffiti. His house on New Bridge Street is now part of a dance-hall. His resting place in Jesmond is largely overgrown with brambles and briars – and a memorial to both his memory and his genius, more singularly inappropriate than one could possibly imagine, is that the city street which is named after him should be one of the ugliest in the whole of Newcastle!

Above: *John Dobson's grave with marble headstone*

Below: *Photograph (below) included by kind permission of Callers-Linden Holdings Limited: (Julia C. Marshall; Linden Hall Hotel, Longhorsley, Northumberland).*

Mr Dobson's funeral

'The interment of the remains of Mr John Dobson took place on Saturday (January 14th) at Jesmond Cemetery, Newcastle, but the ceremony was not attended by such large numbers of the public as might have witnessed the burial of the greatest architect of the North of England, had it not been well known that the relatives of the deceased were anxious for as much privacy as possible in connection with the proceedings.

To a great extent the wish was complied with, however much the fellow townsmen of Mr Dobson might have desired to pay their last respects to his private worth and great professional reputation.

Those, however, who acknowledged him as their chief – the members of the Northern Architectural Association – were not excluded from participating with the family of the deceased in taking part in the obsequies.

The funeral procession departed from Mr Dobson's house, in New Bridge Street, between eleven and twelve o'clock in the morning, in the following order:

Two Mutes
The Hearse

1st Coach – Mr John Dobson, Mr Gibson Kyle, Mr A. Dobson, Mr S. Smirke Jnr., and Mr J. Kyle.

2nd Coach – Mr Gibson Kyle Junr., Rev. W. R. Burnet, Mr John Wardle and Rev. C. A. Raines.

3rd Coach – Mr J. Clayton, Mr P. G. Ellison, Mr Leadbitter and Mr Ralph Dodds.

4th Coach – Mr W. Hawthorn, Dr. Heath, Mr R. Hodgson and Dr. Embleton.

5th Coach – Mr R. R. Dees, Mr Johnstone Hogg and Dr. Saville.

The pall-bearers were Mr J. Clayton, Mr R. Leadbitter, Mr W. Hawthorn, Mr Ralph Dodds, Mr Robert Hodgson and Mr P. G. Ellison.

There were, besides the mourning coaches, about fifteen private carriages and cabs, the Vice-President and several of the members of the Northern Architectural Association being amongst those in the cortège.

On arriving at Jesmond Cemetery, the procession was met by the Rev. W. R. Burnet. The arrangements of the funeral were under the direction of Messrs. T. Sopwith & Co. and Messrs. Moses and Brown, of Newcastle.'

(Ref. *The Newcastle Daily Journal* of 14th January, 1865). Also to be found in that same edition of the Journal is the following notice:

'The Late John Dobson Esquire. Messrs. W. & D. Downey, photographers Eldon Square, in this town, have just published a photographic portrait of the above eminent architect.

It is finished in the above firm's usual style of excellence and is a remarkably correct likeness of the deceased gentleman.'

(Messrs. W. & D. Downey certainly did not believe in 'letting the grass grow under their feet': their advertisement appeared in the *Newcastle Daily Journal* of Monday, January 16th, only two days after John Dobson's interment!)

Period VI 1851–65

Tributes

As a number of writers have seen fit to pay tribute to the genius of John Dobson, I felt it might be both appropriate and illuminating to record their acknowledgements somewhere in my book.

Tom Faulkner (Senior Lecturer in the History of Art and Design, at Newcastle Polytechnic – now Northumbria University) and Andrew Greg (of the Tyne and Wear Museum Service), in their book *John Dobson, Newcastle Architect, 1787–1865*, produced in 1987 to celebrate the bi-centenary of Dobson's birth, make several complimentary references to both Dobson's abilities and his character. While it is not necessary to record every one, perhaps these few examples will suffice to suggest the great esteem in which they held the subject of their book.

> 'A man who contributed more than any other to the architecture of the North-East and Tyneside in particular.
>
> Dobson brought to the region London's most fashionable ideas together with a Geordie's down-to-earth practicality.
>
> Immensely versatile in the range and styles of his buildings, he designed fine houses for the local gentry, noble crescents and squares for the middle classes, hotels and railway stations for travellers, and churches, schools, hospitals, baths and prisons for everyone.
>
> Dobson is a figure of great importance, of whom all of us who live and work in the North-East can justifiably feel proud.'
>
> 'He was an immensely respected and important provincial architect of considerable national renown.'
>
> 'Without doubt the most eminent architect to be born and to have worked in the North-East of England, John Dobson ... has a lengthy career spanning parts of both the Georgian and Victorian epochs.'

And finally,

> 'Dobson was, rightly, as proud of his engineering skills as he was of his architectural designs.'

Lyall Wilkes is another who respected and admired John Dobson's work and the man himself.

Two of his books, *Tyneside Classical* (shared with Gordon Dodds), and *Tyneside Portraits*, mention, in part, the work of Dobson but his 1980 publication, *John Dobson, Architect and Landscape Gardener*, is entirely devoted to the Newcastle architect.

It is from this latter book that I have selected two of Wilkes' commendations:

> 'Dobson's houses were not built for the great and the noble landed families whose houses, executed by Vanbrugh, Adam, Kent or Paine, were built to a scale that created melodramatic palaces in a landscape.
>
> Dobson's houses were built for the country gentry, or for manufacturers or professional men who wished to become gentry.'

In the 'Postscript' to the same book, Wilkes makes this astute observation:

> 'Nothing reflects the spirit of an age more truthfully than its architecture, except, perhaps, its coinage, which also cannot hide debasement.
>
> Visiting a great house by Dobson and seeing the confidence and wealth and belief in the future of which it is an expression, one is compelled to realise that its spirit is as alien to our present age as are the Pyramids ... '

Nikolaus Pevsner, in his 1957 edition of *The Buildings of England: Northumberland*, adds his contribution with the comment:

> 'It was due to Dobson (and Grainger) that the centre of Newcastle became a composition in the best classical taste – well planned, well built and well designed.'

And of Dobson's country houses he adds:

> '... noble designs which establish him at once as one of the best amongst the architects of his generation in England.'

Dr Frank Atkinson, in his book, *Victorian Britain: the North East*, also refers to the Dobson-Grainger partnership in his recognition of Dobson's worth:

> 'John Dobson, architect, partnered by Richard Grainger, the builder, left the face of Newcastle more dramatically and indeed more "laid out" than when he found it ... '

John Burges, in his (1989) book, *The Architects and Architecture of Northumberland and Durham*, has this to say:

> 'Dobson is one of the vital figures in the making of North-Eastern history. (He) remains one of the north-eastern figures who earned prominence in a national setting.'

One unknown writer commented:

> 'John Dobson ... without whose respectable name no history of British architecture could be called complete.'

On p. 87 of his (1914) publication, *Monumental Classical Architecture in Great Britain and Ireland in the nineteenth century*, A. E. Richardson has written:

> 'The general characteristics of Dobson's architecture were adaptability, patience, constructive imagination and intelligence of the "genius loci".'

The Builder, of January 14th, 1865, having learned 'with deep regret' the unexpected death of 'Mr Dobson of Newcastle', goes on to pay him the following tribute:

> 'The versatility of Mr Dobson's talent in turning his hand to work of any kind deserves to be mentioned.
>
> The timber framework used as staiths for shipping coals in the Tyne shows that Mr Dobson was a master of carpentry; the graving-dock, designed for Messrs Smith, at St Peter's shipyard, proved him an engineer; and the warehouses built at the docks at Sunderland and Jarrow, showed that the most massive construction came as easily to his hand as the Gothic churches or luxurious mansions.'

The above is a testimony to John Dobson's abilities, but *The Builder* goes on to refer glowingly to his character:

'We have here given but a meagre sketch of a most industrious and prolific life; but we must not close it without bearing witness to Mr Dobson's upright conduct as a man and his generous and kindly nature.

The profession has lost a very eminent member and Newcastle a distinguished and most respected citizen.'

Further proof of Dobson's integrity and the esteem in which he was held by his peers is demonstrated by his involvement in 'The High Level Bridge project':

'The construction of the High Level Bridge ... involved an immense destruction of house-property; and here Mr Dobson's services were called into requisition in the settlement of compensation to the owners of the property destroyed. His knowledge of its value, the implicit confidence placed by the owners and occupiers in his honesty and impartiality, enabled Mr Dobson ... to adjust all the claims for compensation without carrying (with one exception) any of the claims into a court of law – in the settlement of all kinds of disputes ... the sound judgement and dispassionate temperament of Mr Dobson were successful in extinguishing litigation.'

The Newcastle Daily Chronicle of Monday, January 9th 1865 carried the following report of John Dobson's death:

'We regret to announce the unexpected death of John Dobson Esq., architect, which took place at his house in New Bridge Street, Newcastle, at nine o'clock yesterday morning. Mr Dobson, since the year 1863, had retired from the active pursuit of his profession and had sought change of air, in failing health, in the neighbouring village of Ryton.

Mr Dobson returned to Newcastle a few days ago and from that time to the present his health had been gradually sinking and had given rise to some apprehension on the part of his friends, though a fatal termination was not immediately apprehended. He was in full tide of prosperity and usefulness, when a stroke of paralysis cut him down in the full vigour of his intellect and though he had rallied considerably from the first effects of this attack, he had never been himself since.

Mr Dobson leaves two sons and two daughters, but he leaves no successor to his professional reputation in his own family.

His youngest son, who was educated in his father's office, was a youth of great promise and gained the prizes at King's College, London, in Professor Donaldson's architectural class, both for the theory and practice of architecture – a most unusual combination.

Mr A. R. Dobson was unfortunately killed by the great explosion which took place in Gateshead, on the 6th October, 1854.

One of Mr Dobson's daughters is married to Mr Sidney Smirke R.A., the eminent architect in London, by whom some of Mr Dobson's works have been continued.'

The Newcastle Daily Journal, also of January 9th, has this to say:

'A general feeling of regret was felt in Newcastle yesterday when the tidings spread that Mr John Dobson, our talented and renowned architect, had expired at an early hour in the morning.

The deceased had not, for a considerable time past, taken an active part in the arduous duties pertaining to his profession, old age and failing strength having incapacitated him from so doing.

He had long been an invalid and has gone to his final rest, in his 78th year, full of honours and with the regret of a numerous and attached body of friends and admirers.

Mr Dobson's funeral

Few men have survived for so long a period the wear and tear incident to the profession which Mr Dobson so successfully followed.'

The Newcastle Daily Journal, in its obituary for John Dobson, printed on the 9th January, 1865, had this to say:

'... there are few buildings of any note, in this town, or in Northumberland, with which his name is not, in some way, associated.

Possessed of genius of the highest order, he has done a great work in reviving Church architecture in this neighbourhood; and of the many fine examples of his taste and skill, in this branch of his profession, Newcastle may be justly proud, while the versatility of his talent is shown by the erection of buildings from his designs, adapted for almost every purpose.'

A week later, in the edition of January 16th, this same newspaper concluded:

'... it may be questioned whether any architect, in London or the provinces, has ever designed and carried out such a number of buildings and of such a miscellaneous character.

Mr Dobson's genius was not confined to any one particular branch of architecture; but whatever description of buildings he had to erect his ability was displayed both in its design, to mark its purpose, and in adapting its internal arrangements most effectively for its requirements.

Some of his erections are more of an engineering character than architectural, yet even in these he was equally successful.'

The Builder of January 14th, 1865, paid this tribute;

'A history of Mr Dobson's works would be the history of nearly every territorial residence in the Country.'

John Grundy and Grace McCombie, writing in Pevsner and Richmond's 1992 edition of *The Buildings of England: Northumberland*, have written:

'The most prominent and most talented of the group of the pantheon of local architects who emerged in the early part of the nineteenth century.'

Referring to Dobson's Greek Doric design of the Royal Jubilee School (Newcastle), in 1810, the two writers continue:

'Over the next quarter of a century Dobson continued to use the (Doric) style with an increasing freedom and sophistication which places him among the best architects of his generation in the whole of England.'

These are all glowing and richly deserved tributes, indicative of the esteem and affection in which John Dobson was rightly held both by contemporaries and those who, since, have written of his work.

But perhaps it is fitting that the final words (a tribute to his character rather than the fine quality of his workmanship) should be those of his daughter, Margaret Jane, who, in her *Memoir* of 1885, had this to say:

'He never exceeded an estimate and never had a legal dispute with a contractor.'

ADDENDA

Bolton Hall, West Bolton, Alnwick, Northumberland

Bolton Hall *(West Bolton, Alnwick, Northumberland)*

A monastery once stood on the site of the south garden. This was 'dissolved' at the time of the Reformation. The site was then occupied, in the 17th c. by a domestic farmhouse. In the 18th c. it became a dower-house for Shawdon Hall. At the beginning of the 19th c. John Dobson added the plain, classical south front. Photographed by kind permission of Mr and Mrs J. H. Young.

Bolton Hall. The five-bay south front with sash windows and a hipped roof.

Bolton Hall, facing east

The Old Vicarage ('Mill Race House'), Netherwitton

The Old Vicarage ('Mill Race House', Netherwitton)

The Old Vicarage, Netherwitton is included in John Dobson's list of works, published in the *Newcastle Daily Journal* of January 16th, 1865. Unfortunately the newspaper makes no reference to the nature of Dobson's work, neither does it say for whom the work was done or when. Photographed by kind permission of Mrs J. C. R. Trevelyan of Netherwitton Hall.

The Old Vicarage (Netherwitton)

Bibliography

Margaret Jane Dobson, *A Memoir of John Dobson*, Lambert and Co., Newcastle, 1885.

Tom Faulkner and Andrew Greg, *John Dobson, Newcastle Architect, 1787–1865*, Tyne and Wear Museums Service, 1987.

Nikolaus Pevsner, *The Buildings of England: Northumberland*, Penguin, 1957.

Pevsner and Richmond, *The Buildings of England: Northumberland*, Penguin, 1992.

W. W. Tomlinson, *Comprehensive Guide to Northumberland*, W. H. Robinson, 11th. Edition.

Lyall Wilkes, *John Dobson, Architect and Landscape Gardener*, Oriel Press, 1980.

Bruce Allsopp and Ursula Clark, *Historic Architecture of Northumberland and Newcastle upon Tyne*, Oriel Press, 1977.

Stanley Prins and Roger Massingberd-Mundy ed., *A Guide to the Anglican Churches in Newcastle and Northumberland*, Newcastle Diocesan Bishop's Editorial Committee of THE LINK, 1982.

Frank Graham, *The Old Halls, Houses and Inns of Northumberland*, 1977.

Frank Graham, *Tynedale from Blanchland to Carter Bar*, 1978.

Robert Hugill, *Castles and Peles of the English Border*, Frank Graham, 1970.

Lyall Wilkes and Gordon Dodds, *Tyneside Classical*, John Murray, 1964.

Lyall Wilkes, *Tyneside Portraits*, Frank Graham, 1971.

Pevsner and Williamson, *The Buildings of England: County Durham*, Penguin, 1983.

The Revd. J. Hodgson and Mr F. C. Laird, *The Beauties of England and Wales*, Vol 12, pt. 1, Northumberland and Nottinghamshire, 1813.

Tyne and Wear County Council Museums, *The Tyneside Classical Tradition; Classical Architecture in the North East c.* 1700–1850, published to accompany the Exhibition held at the Laing Art Gallery, Newcastle upon Tyne, 15th July–17th August, 1980.

David Bean, *Newcastle 900: A Portrait of Newcastle upon Tyne*, Newcastle upon Tyne City Council for Newcastle, 900, 1980.

Peter Winter and David Milne, Jonathan Brown, Alan Rushworth, *Newcastle upon Tyne*, Northern Heritage Consultancy Ltd., 1989.

T. H. Rowland, *Waters of Tyne*, T. H. Rowland, 1991.

Thomas Faulkner and Phoebe Lowery, *Lost Houses of Newcastle and Northumberland*, Jill Raines, 1996.

David Crystal, *Cambridge Biographical Encyclopedia*, Cambridge University Press, 1995.

P. Anderson Graham, *Highways and Byways in Northumbria*, MacMillan and Co., 1920.

Neville Whittaker, *The Old Halls and Manor Houses of Durham*, Frank Graham, 1975.

Frank Graham, *Newcastle upon Tyne: Sixty Views from Old Prints and Original Drawings*, Frank Graham, 1984.

T. H. Rowland, *Discovering Northumberland*, Frank Graham, 1973.

Arthur Mee, *The King's England: Northumberland*, C. L. S. Linnell, revised and ed., Hodder and Stoughton, 1964.

Frank Atkinson, *Victorian Britain: The North East*, David and Charles, 1989.

Period VI 1851–65

Sydney Middlebrook, *Newcastle upon Tyne: Its Growth and Achievements*, S.R. Publishers Ltd., reprint, 1968.

H. L. Honeyman, *Northumberland*, County Books Series, Robert Hale Ltd., 1949.

M. J. Jackson, *Castles of Northumbria*, Barmkin Books, 1992.

Mike Kirkup, *Was There Ever a Railway Row? A History of North Seaton Colliery and Village*, Woodhorn Press, 1997.

George MacDonald Fraser, *The Steel Bonnets*, Pan books, 1974.

Peter Meadows and Edward Waterson, *Lost Houses of County Durham*, Jill Rames, 1993.

Neville Whittaker and Ursula Clark, *Historic Architecture of County Durham*, Oriel Press, 1971.

William Parson and William White, *History, Directory and Gazetteer of the Counties of Durham and Northumberland*, Vols. 1 and 2, Edward Baines and Son, Leeds Mercury Office, 1827 and 1828

F. W. Manders, *History of Gateshead*, 1973.

Department of the Environment, *An Historical, Topographical and Descriptive View of the County Palatine of Durham*, Vol. 1, Mackenzie and Ross, 1834.

Department of the Environment, *A List of Buildings of Special Architectural or Historic Interest: District of Gateshead*, Department of the Environment, 1987.

Department of the Environment, *A List of Buildings of Special Architectural or Historic Interest: District of Newcastle, Tyne and Wear*, Department of the Environment, 1987.

Howard Colvin, *A Biographical Dictionary of British Architects, 1600–1840*, John Murray, 1978.

Anon, *Ward's Dictionary for Newcastle, including Gateshead, Shields and Sunderland*, R. Ward and Sons, 1915–16.

Robert Hugill, *Castles of Durham*, Frank Graham, 1979.

G. M. Trevelyan, *Grey of Fallodon*, Longmans Green and Co., 1937.

Frank Graham, *The Bridges of Northumberland and Durham*, Frank Graham, 1975.

John Hodgson, *A History of Morpeth* (Frank Graham's facsimile edition of Hodgson's original 1832 publication), 1973.

A. H. Tweddle, *Town Trail for Morpethians*, (Series), A. H. Tweddle, 1984.

Oswin Craster, *A History of Embleton Parish Church* (Photography by George Skipper, Designed by Sue Dale) n.d.

David Lovie, *The Buildings of Grainger Town: Four Townscape Walks around Newcastle*, (English Partnerships), 1997.

Anon., *The Newcastle Daily Journal*, various editions.

Anon., *The Newcastle Daily Chronicle*, various editions.

Anon., *The Newcastle Courant*, various editions.

Anon., *The Tyne Mercury*, various editions.

The following books were used by Miss Carol Ward in her thesis on 'The Leazes' (Hexham), which she very graciously allowed me to borrow and make extensive use of:

Andrew Jackson Downing, *The Architecture of Country Houses* 1816–52, Da Capo, 1968.

Mark Girouard, *Life in the English Country House*, Yale University Press, 1978.

Jill Franklin, *The Gentleman's Country House, 1835–1914*, Routledge and Kegan Paul, 1981.

Martin Page, *Historic Houses Restored and Preserved*, Whitney Library of Design, 1979.

Frank Graham, *Historic Newcastle*, Frank Graham, 1976.

Index of buildings illustrated

Acton House, Felton 80
All Saints Church, Monkwearmouth 215
Almshouses, Hospital of St Mary the Virgin, Newcastle 225–6
Angerton Hall, Morpeth 78
Archibald Reed Monument, The, Newcastle 194
Axwell park, Blaydon 42–3

Backworth Hall, Backworth 36
Baptist Church, The, Howard Street, North Shields 207
Barber Surgeons' Hall, Newcastle 225
Beaufront Castle, Hexham 186–8
Belford Hall, Northumberland 51–4
Bellister Castle, Haltwhistle 96–7
Benfieldside Vicarage, Shotley Bridge 227–9
Benwell Tower 141–2
Blagdon Hall, Blagdon 70–1
Blenkinsopp Hall, Haltwhistle 156
Boldon House, East Boldon 186
Bolton Hall, Alnwick 275–6
Bradley Hall, Wylam 27–9
Brinkburn Priory Church, Northumberland 161–4
Brinkburn Priory House, Northumberland 164–6
Burnhopeside Hall, Lanchester 136

Carlton Terrace, Newcastle 185
(Castle) Keep, The, Newcastle
    See Keep (Castle), The Newcastle
Cathedral Church of St Nicholas
    See St Nicholas' Cathedral Church, Newcastle
Central Station, Newcastle 218, 264
Chantry, The, Morpeth 98–9
Chatton Bridge, Chatton 246
Cheeseburn Grange, Stamfordham 23–25
Chesters, Humshaugh 138, 169–70
Chipchase Castle, Wark-on-Tyne 60–2
Chollerton Grange, Hexham 134, 208

Church of St Andrew, The, Bywell, Stocksfield 129, 221
Church of St Andrew, The, Winston on Tees 215
Church of St Cuthbert, The, Benfieldside, Shotley Bridge 220–1
Church of St Cuthbert, The, Gateshead 211–12
Church of St Cuthbert, The, Greenhead 106
Church of St Gregory, The, Kirknewton 258–9
Church of St James, The, Benwell, Newcastle 153
Church of St John the Baptist, The, Grainger Street, Newcastle 123, 213, 242, 256
Church of St John the Baptist, The, Meldon 216
Church of St John of Beverley, The, Hexham 49
Church of St Lawrence, Warkworth 258
Church of St Mary the Virgin, The, Gateshead 239
Church of St Mary the Virgin, The, Stamfordham 212
Church of St Michael and All Angels, The, Ford 235–9
Church of St Michael and All Angels, The, Houghton-le-Spring 254–5
Church of St Nicholas, West Boldon 133
Church of St Paul, The, Holme Eden 205–6
Church of St Paul, The, High Elswick, Newcastle 253
Church of St Peter, The, Bywell 217
Church of St Thomas the Martyr, The, Newcastle 131–33
Church of The Holy Trinity, The, Embleton 213
Clayton Memorial Church, The
    See Jesmond Parish Church
Clayton Street, Newcastle 179
Collingwood Monument, The, Tynemouth 209
Cordwainers' Hall, The, Newcastle 178
Court House, Morpeth 109–11

281

Period VI 1851–65

Craster Tower, Northumberland 179–81

Doxford Hall, Chathill 47–8

Eldon Square, Newcastle 152
Embleton Old Vicarage, Embleton (now Embleton Towers) 116–120

Fallodon Hall, Embleton 29–31
Fish Market, The, Newcastle 91–2
Flotterton House, Rothbury 77

Gosforth Park, Newcastle 55
Grainger Market, The, Newcastle 157–8
Grainger Town, John Dobson and the Streets of 173–7
(14–20) Great North Road, Newcastle 137
Grey Street, 'The Curve', Newcastle 167
Grey Street (East Side), Newcastle 161

Hackwood House, Hexham 195
Hall, The, Glanton Pyke, Glanton, Alnwick 125–6
Harbottle Castle (House), Northumberland 124–5
Haughton Castle, Hexham 198–201
Hawthorn Tower, Easington 75
Hebburn Hall, Hebburn 59
Hermitage, The, Hexham 62–4
Hexham Abbey, Hexham 247–8
Hexham House 59–60
High Ford Bridge, Morpeth 107–9
Holeyn Hall, Wylam 249–50
Holme Eden Abbey, Warwick Bridge 171–73
Holme Eden Vicarage, Warwick Bridge 206
Holy Trinity Church, Gateshead 168–9
Holy Trinity Vicarage, Seghill 244

Jesmond Parish Church, Newcastle 259–60
John Dobson's grave 266
John Dobson's house, Newcastle 79

Keep (Castle), The, Newcastle 210, 240–41
Keeper's Cottage, The, Horsely-on-the-Hill 214

Lambton Castle, Durham 261–4
Leazes, The, Hexham 232–5
Lilburn Tower, Alnwick 113–16
Longhirst Hall, Morpeth 102–5
Low Ford Bridge, Morpeth 160–1
Lying-in Hospital, The, Newcastle 90

Linden Hall, Longhorsley 21–3

Market Keeper's Cottage/House, Newcastle 190–2
Mechanics' Institute, North Shields 247
Meldon Park, Morpeth 139
Minsteracres Monastery, Consett 37, 196
Mitford Hall, Mitford 101–2

Navigational Beacons, The, Ross Sands 65–7
Nazareth House, Newcastle 41
Nelson Street, Newcastle 178
'New Bridge', The, Morpeth 142–51
Newbrough Hall, Hexham 20
Newcastle General Cemetery, Jesmond, Newcastle 158–60
Newton Hall (now Mowden Hall School), Stocksfield 229, 231
Newton Villa Farm, Morpeth 67
North Seaton Hall, near Ashington 26–7
Nunnykirk Hall, Netherwitton, Morpeth 88–9
Nun Street, Newcastle 177

Old Vicarage, The ('Longstone House'), Chatton 202–4
Old Vicarage, The, Haltwhistle 92
Old Vicarage, The, Netherwitton 276–7
Old Vicarage, The, Ponteland 65
Old Vicarage, The, Stamfordham 208

Percy Chapel, The, Tynemouth Priory 230–1
Pineapple Inn, The, High Chirton, North Shields 8
Prestwick Lodge, Ponteland 33–5
Prison, The, Wooler 76

Rock Hall, Alnwick 57–8
R.C. Church of St Elizabeth See Minsteracres Monastery
(Royal) Station Hotel, Newcastle 226–7

St Andrew's Church, Newcastle 197
St Columba's Presbyterian Church, North Shields 245
St John's Church, Otterburn 245
St Joseph's R.C. Church, Birtley 193
St Mary's Church, Gateshead 233a
St Mary's Parish Church, Belford 111–13
St Mary's Place, Newcastle 122
St Nicholas' Cathedral, Newcastle 40, 84–88, 100, 153–5, 255

Index of buildings illustrated

St Nicholas' Church, South Gosforth 56–7
St Thomas' Crescent, Newcastle 129
Sandhoe House, Hexham 207
Scottish Presbyterian Church, The, North Shields 19
Shawdon Hall, Alnwick 90–1, 250–3
Sheriff Hill Hall, Gateshead Fell 80–84
South Lodge, Belford Hall 71

Thirston House, Morpeth 68–9
Town Hall, The, North Shields 201
Trinity House, Newcastle 188–90

Tynemouth Castle 41–2

Unthank Hall, Haltwhistle 32–3, 257

Village Cross, The, Holy Island 121

Wallington Hall, Cambo, Morpeth 50, 242–4
Watergate Building, The, Newcastle 135–6
(West) Jesmond Towers, Newcastle 38–9, 93–5
Woolsington Hall, Ponteland 130
Wynyard Park, Billingham 140–41